ENDORSEMENTS

Once we understand the times, order, and purposes that God is bringing from heaven, then we will see a new authority begin to arise in each of us, individually and corporately. This corporateness is called the Church, the ecclesia. This authority will cause us to be able to overthrow the enemies that have resisted us in past seasons. God will reveal new strategies of warfare that we have not considered before. With those new strategies, we will have a new place of authority in our territories.

The Corporate Armor, by Jacquie Tyre, not only looks at us individually but as a tribe that makes up a troop. There are certain things that will not be accomplished until we have come into the unity of the faith. This book will help us get there.

Dr. Chuck D. Pierce
President, Glory of Zion International Ministries
President, Global Spheres, Inc.

Jacquie Tyre, Susan, and I have been friends it seems for as long as I can remember. More so, we have become warriors together. Standing side by side, we have come to rely on each other for everything from simple kindness to the covering of prayer. Together, we have learned to ⸺k in spiritual realities that we may not fully understand ⸺ne immediacy of the moment. In applying God's truth as He reveals it, however, we acquire knowledge through experience and strength through battle.

Thus, it is with deep confidence that I heartedly recommend Jacquie's book, *The Corporate Armor*. Jacquie takes a well-understood subject and brings it to a whole new level. Most Christians understand that the armor of God as presented in Ephesians is their personal protection for spiritual battle, indeed for their spiritual survival. What they don't realize is how this same equipping of Holy Spirit applies to the church, not as an option but a necessity.

Our battles are ever-present. Our equipping for battle is a process. Victory is assured, but victory requires training. We call this growth. Want to know why you succeed at times and fail at other times? Want to know how to lead not only yourself or your family, but entire people groups to greater levels of success? It starts here, applying a truth we once thought was only for individuals.

Let us answer the question that Jacquie poses early in her book: "This is good and it is right…but is that all?"

No, that is not all. This book is the next chapter in our growth as warriors, as kings, and as a church triumphant.

Clay Nash
Minister/ Author
Clay Nash Ministries

Jed Clampett was the lead character on a famous TV show called *The Beverly Hillbillies* which aired in the 1960s. A few lines from the show's theme song came to my mind as I read Jacquie Tyre's book, *The Corporate Armor*. The words go like this, "Then one day he was shootin' at some food, and up through the ground came a bubblin' crude. Oil that is...black gold...Texas tea." I don't think Jacquie was shootin' at some food but I do believe she has struck oil.

This book is one of those that has the potential to help shift the church back into what Jesus had in his mind when he said, "I will build my Church." (ref. Matthew 16:18). Much of Western modern-day Christianity has somehow shifted the Church into a place to where the Gospel is all about the individual when clearly that was never the intention of Jesus. Even in ancient biblical Hebrew culture we know this is not the fact. Remember Achan? (Joshua 7:1) This powerful book, *The Corporate Armor*, is written in a way that will help us realign with Jesus' original idea—the whole; the body!

I encourage you to read this book with an open heart, and allow Holy Spirit to impart the wisdom with these pages to you. This book will change the way you look and relate to not only the church, but the five-fold ministry of the apostle, prophet, evangelist, pastor and teacher. Please, don't just read this book but share it. It's a tool for awakening. This is a Kingdom book.

Dr. Greg Hood, Th.D.
Apostolic Leader, Global Reformation Ministries
President, Kingdom University
Author of: *Rebuilding The Broken Altar*
www.GregHood.org
www.KingdomU.org

Apostle Jacquie Tyre, senior leader of CityGate Atlanta Kingdom Center located in Peachtree Corners, Georgia, has released a trumpet-like clarion call for the Body of Christ to come into biblically defined corporality. In today's culture of extreme individualism, self-interest, and personal pursuits, this well written and engaging book unveils the power and influence of authentic, Biblical corporality. Our scriptural faith is both individual and corporate. This is clearly what the Apostle Paul taught when he referred to each individual follower of Christ as a 'temple' of the Holy Spirit, and the corporate Church also as a 'temple' of God. The author is teaching us we can embrace our individuality without ignoring our corporality as the people of God.

I am convinced this volume will serve as a serious update on the vital subject of spiritual warfare. In light of what's happening in the world today, this equipping manual could not have been released at a better time! Weary intercessors and Kingdom leaders will be educated and encouraged as they and we face increasingly greater challenges in all we are called to do in Jesus' name.

Jacquie has released fresh revelation about the protective armor that is available to us as we confront and overcome the "world-forces of darkness" and advance the agenda of the Kingdom of God on the earth. I know of no other teaching and writing that connects the spiritual armor for the believer and the corporate church with the five-fold ministry gifts given us by our ascended and enthroned King Jesus! (ref. Ephesians 4:11). This is amazing revelation and transformative understanding!

Whether you are a new follower of the Lord Jesus or a seasoned leader, you will greatly benefit and grow by embracing the insights and lessons this book affords. Use it for personal study and for teaching others.

Jim Hodges
Founder and President
Federation of Ministers and Churches International

God has given Jacquie incredible insight and a present word for the ekklesia and if we will heed it, pray, and press in to it, everything will shift. The revelation in this book releases corporate anointing at a higher level, resulting in greater authority for Christ's Kingdom purposes. I love Ephesians 6 and this book presents the armor of God in a fresh way that should encourage each of us to embrace and participate and yes, overtake the enemies' schemes. Highly recommend!

Tim Sheets
Author of *Angel Armies, Angel Armies on Assignment, Planting the Heavens*
Tim Sheets Ministries
The Oasis Church, Middletown, Ohio
www.timsheets.org
www.oasiswired.org

What Apostle Jacquie Tyre has done in her book *The Corporate Armor*, is so very rare, and that is to provide Biblical revelation that creates a narrative that we've never seen before. Wow! I am blown away! Her Holy Spirit revelation concerning the operation of the armor of

God as being corporate is a truth I've never seen, but I am in full agreement with. Then, for Apostle Tyre to make the direct connection of each of the Five-Fold Offices being linked to a piece of armor and demonstrate the function thereof in the ekklesia, is astounding.

I say with great humility as a Bible student for 36 years, thank you Apostle Jacquie Tyre for sharing with us this Holy Spirit revelation that will forever change the way we look at and engage in the Armor of God!

This book, *The Corporate Armor*, is number one on my "must have list," as a Pastor and Bible teacher.

Dr. Dwain Miller
President Dwain Miller Ministries Inc.
Senior Pastor Cross Life Church of Little Rock, AR

Jacquie Tyre's book, *The Corporate Armor*, is a fascinating look at the spiritual armor of Ephesians 6 as not only individual armament but as weaponry for the ekklesia as a corporate Body. I couldn't put it down! This revolutionary understanding will equip the church to effectively push back the gates of hell, shift from defensive to offensive positioning and advance the Kingdom of God on the earth.

Jane Hamon
Co-Apostle, Vision Church @ Christian International
Author: *Dreams and Visions, The Deborah Company, The Cyrus Decree, Discernment,* and *Declarations for Breakthrough*
www.tomandjanehamon.com

The Corporate Armor, by Apostle Jacquie Tyre, flies in the face of the individualistic cultural attitudes of much of Western society, reintroducing the reader to the forgotten corporate culture and mindset that the Bible was written in. This life changing book unmasks the mystery and power of the corporation anointing through God's ekklessia for the purpose of advancing the Kingdom in a territory. The book is a prophetic roadmap that we are "safer, better and more anointed together" than we can ever be under the banner of our personal gifting ad calling. With the forensic aptitude of a seasoned biblical scholar, Apostle Jacquie gives the reader the most unusual perspective on Ephesians 6:10-18 that I have ever heard. I highly encourage you add this book to your arsenal of books!

Dr. Francis Myles
Author: *The Order of Melchizedek* and *Issuing Divine Restraining Orders from the Courts of Heaven*
www.francismyles.com

I would recommend *The Corporate Armor* to every leader in the Body of Christ. If embraced, it will increase the effectiveness of communication and execution of the mission the Lord has assigned us to unlock and establish kingdom. This alignment creating the foundation of corporate protection that is within our reach will propel us forward in every area of ministry to bring forth a great harvest. Previous generations have not had access to many of the greatest blessings the Lord died to give us. It is also a great book for those that are curious about the apostolic paradigm and will answer many questions and releases clarity concerning its function. Jacquie has done a wonderful job of putting her shoulder to the wheel and waiting on the Lord to hear what He is saying. She has written simply and clearly in just the way He speaks. Jacquie's walk with the Lord in authenticity and honesty has brought forth revelation to expand the foundation upon which the Lord will build His house. I treasure the gift of God within her that she humbly and freely gives.

Anne S. Tate
International Director of Prayer and the Watches
Glory of Zion, International
www.gloryofzion.org

In this unique and thoroughly digestible treatise on *The Corporate Armor*, Jacquie Tyre has gifted the Body of Christ a remarkable jewel of revelation. Correctly understood and applied, it will transform the role and impact of God's ekklesia in the world. In short, it is a manifesto for the prophetic fulfillment and apostolic success that the Bible promises the end time church directly preceding Christ's return. Truth once seen can never be unseen. Thank you, Jacquie, for opening our eyes to see.

Kevin and Rose Sambrook
Apostolic Ministers, Rhema Restoration Ministries, Northern Ireland

---

I have known Jacquie Tyre for many years, and I consider her to be a seasoned warrior of prayer and intercession. She is like a general in God's army, and this book is like a tactical manual for spiritual combat. I especially urge groups of intercessors to study it together. As evil rises in our generation, and divisiveness increases, the church must develop greater unity in prayer. Corporate unity is the heart of this book, and the secret to victory. This book will help churches and prayer groups to align so that we can reach maximum effectiveness.

J. Lee Grady
Author and Director of The Mordecai Project
themordecaiproject.org

In *The Corporate Armor*, Jacquie Tyre writes with the authority of an Apostle, the foresight of a prophet, the clarity of a teacher, the passion of an evangelist, and the compassion of a pastor. It is both insightful and insightful, leading us into deep revelation and provoking us to action.

Many with as strong a prophetic word as hers, seem to communicate disdain for the church. However, as Jacquie challenges the church and status quo, she does so with a deep love for the body of Christ as a community and as a ruling ekklesia in a way that demonstrates God's heart and destiny for the church. And in a time where unity is banded around to support myriad causes, Jacquie deftly illustrates with profound understanding and spiritual perception what a truly united church can be and is able to accomplish.

With her expert knowledge and experience in how we can fit together in correct placement and alignment,

Jacquie is a master Chiropractor for the body of Christ. The adjustment she administers in *The Corporate Armor* will help us move unhindered in our purpose, gifts, and assignments from God.

Joel Balin
Associate Pastor, Cobb Vineyard
Author of *The Spirit, Soul, and Body of Worship*, and co-author of *War on Fear*.

The Lord is flooding His church, the ekklesia, with fresh revelation and insight as we have entered into a new era of His kingdom and His will being carried out on the earth. Jacquie Tyre carries in her heart one of those revelations regarding the armor of God. This message shook me to the core and has given me fresh insight into the power and might that God has provided for His church. The armor of God has been a primary teaching in the body of Christ which releases an understanding of who we are as warriors for the Lord and the divine protection He provides for us, but *The Corporate Armor* takes us exponentially into a new realm of understanding the five-fold gifting from Jesus in Ephesians 4 and its inseparable link to the armor. This book will stir you up.

Dr. Thomas Schlueter
Prince of Peace House of Prayer – Pastor
Texas Apostolic Prayer Network
www.tomschlueter.com

Jacquie Tyre is a kingdom leader of integrity. I have known her for 25 years both as a member of my congregation and as a pastor in our city. Jacquie is a fierce kingdom warrior and her new book is a force to be reckoned with. Her insights not only into the book of Ephesians, but into the call of Christ to walk in kingdom authority are significant. I believe she is accurate when she says the entire book of Ephesians builds toward the church's authority in Christ, represented in the seven pieces of spiritual armor. When she links the five equipping gifts of apostle, pastor, evangelist, preacher and teacher to the seven pieces of armor, it gives traction to the church to be the prevailing church which Christ is building that will push back the gates of hell. In a day when all too many pastors are shrinking in fear, Jacquie Tyre issues a wakeup call to stand strong and occupy the land. Every leader needs a leader, and Jacquie has become one of mine.

Fred A. Hartley III
Lead Pastor Lilburn Alliance Church
President College of Prayer International
www.college of prayer.org

Some gifted leaders receive revelation from God. Still, Apostle Jacquie is the embodiment of the revelation God has given her in her new book *The Corporate Armor*. One of the primary purposes of an apostle is to release an apostolic anointing upon the corporate church so that every believer functions from an apostolic perspective. The apostolic deposit from this book provides applicable illumination for understanding how God wants to use authentic five-fold gifts to sustain and protect the rapidly growing awakening revival enveloping the earth. This book is a gift from God to "RESET" our approach to global spiritual conquest. All must read it.

Yul Crawford
Prophet, Atlanta, GA

Reading the commentaries and devotionalization of spiritual warfare, we would think Paul was more interested in Roman armaments than God's. The descriptions of the imprisoned apostle sitting chained between two wardens, observing a Roman soldier, inspired by that portrait, leave out the essential reality that Paul never wrote by his own inspiration.

No, Paul is revealing how things really work in the spirit. Paul describes actual spiritual realities and communicates in metaphors about God's weaponry. Paul does not ask us to study Romans. Instead, he brings us into revelation.

Jacquie Tyre starts where Paul starts, communicates from Paul's revelation, and concludes where Paul does. That will bring revelation into your life more than an exciting, enjoyable examination of Roman history.

The sword of the Lord is God's rhema that arrives with the power to make it happen. The weapons are not defensive because Paul says they become available when we engage, wrestle, overcome, and displace hell!

The revelation—that the spiritual warfare picture puts the weapons of God in an array on the ekklesia—will alter your battle-plan perspective. However, it does no damage to the apparent truth that God equips you with personally while positioning your spiritual experience of conflict within the kingdom where it properly belongs.

Yes, you will read this more than once with profit. Yes, you will put it on the shelf marked "classics." Yes, you say, "This is a book needed for the New Era."

Thank God for this revelation and this seasoned apostle's expertise and experience in faithful, consistent pressing for God's purposes by usurping the usurpers.

Dr. Don Lynch
Founder, Ministry Matrix
Kingdom Leadership Institute,
Freedom Ministry and Freedom House
www.Drdnlynch.com

The Corporate Armor

The title of this book lays the foundation for what the Lord is releasing in the body of Christ today. We are being aligned and armored into the full expression of the ekklesia like never before. This book helps lay a great foundation but also empowers you to see the opportunities that are before you as you step into and put on the Armor of the Lord

The word that I quote here "The belt of truth speaks of guarding against error, compromise, or deception infiltrating the life of the Church, as individual members and also for the corporate body." This statement empowers us for movement as we embrace our aligned identity to the truth of the word.

I encourage you to read and then reread this book so you as the reader can grasp you place in the corporate identity in the Lord.

Pat McManus
Apostle, Kingdom Impact Center, Aurora, Illinois

THE CORPORATE ARMOR

GOD'S DESIGN FOR THE VICTORIOUS CHURCH

Jacquie Tyre

JACQUIE TYRE

COPYRIGHT

The Corporate Armor

Copyright © 2021 by Jacquie Tyre

All rights reserved. This book is protected by the copyright laws of the United States of America. This book may not be copied or reprinted for commercial gain or profit. The use of short quotations or occasional page copying for personal or group study is encouraged. Permission will be granted upon request from Jacquie Tyre. All rights reserved. Any emphasis added to Scripture quotations is the author's own.

Unless otherwise noted, scripture quotations are taken from the New American Standard Bible (NASB) and the New American Standard Bible 1995 (NASB 1995).

Edit/Layout by Jim Bryson (JamesLBryson@gmail.com)

Cover design by David Munoz (davidmunoznvtn@gmail.com)

Dedication

I wish to dedicate this work to the rising remnant warriors that are coming up out of the hidden places in search of finding their place of alignment; to those who have caught a glimpse of the promises and purposes of Christ through His ekklesia; to those who passionately desire to see the kingdom of God advanced on earth; and to those who know in the depth of their being that we, as the church, are to move victoriously as one body, fully armored to go into the enemy's territory to rescue the perishing, set captives free, heal the sick, and deliver the tormented. To all my fellow kingdom warriors, I dedicate this book for the advancement of Christ and His kingdom and the protection that comes from being fully armored with the very armor of God.

Acknowledgments

First of all, I want to thank my husband, Mike, for all the years of support and encouragement you have given as I have persistently pursued the Lord and His call upon my life. I would not be who I am today without you and the journey we have made together. Thank you for challenging me to not settle for what is but to press on to what can be. Thank you for loving and faithfully walking with me, even when things were tough. We are truly better together!

Abundant thanks must also be given to those who have steadfastly believed in me and the message contained in these pages: Dutch Sheets, Clay Nash, Greg Hood, Anne Tate, and countless others. I am humbled by your support and encouragement.

Words cannot begin to adequately express the depth of my gratitude to our CityGate Atlanta leaders and shareholders. The many ways you have come along on this journey of learning how to walk out this revelation has been invaluable. We are on a great adventure together and the best is yet to come!

For all those from across the nation and beyond, who have sent notes of encouragement to spur me on.

Thank you!

TABLE OF CONTENTS

Foreword	1
Introduction	5
Section 1 - God's Armor of Protection	9
1 The Armor of God	11
2 The Church Jesus Is Building	23
3 United and Protected	39
4 Armored by Christ's Leadership Anointings	49
Section 2 - The Corporate Armor	57
5 Apostles and Prophets	59
6 Evangelist	77
7 Pastor-Shepherd	91
8 Teacher	101
9 The Sword of the Spirit	111
10 Concluding Thoughts	123
About the Author	129
Contact Info	131

Foreword

by Dutch Sheets

I ALWAYS FIND IT ENCOURAGING to watch individuals mature in their walk with God and a revelation of His ways. It stretches and inspires me to do likewise, providing a reminder that when it comes to spiritual growth, one never "arrives." Jacquie Tyre is striking this chord for me once again.

Ceci and I have known Jacquie for 20 or more years—we'll just leave the number there so as not to hint at the true ages of our incredibly young-looking appearances. Our mutual involvement in the prayer movement of the past couple of decades produced many opportunities to interact and work together. This provided a front-row seat as Holy Spirit performed His maturation process in us. For years I knew Jacquie was a strong intercessor and passionate worshipper; then, I was able to hear her balanced, in-depth teaching. Even more recently,

I've watched her move in strong prophetic and apostolic graces. Jacquie is very well-rounded and diverse in her spiritual gifting.

And now, thankfully, she is writing.

When I first heard Jacquie relate a small portion of the revelation you're about to read, I distinctly remember thinking: *Where did that come from? I've not heard those insights before.* I actually stated that it needed to be in a book, to which she smiled and responded, "I'm working on it."

And here it is.

Biblical truth, like many subjects, foods, and even the earth, exists in layers that must be uncovered and explored in order to discover all of its many facets. As an example, I recall my math-learning days. Just when I thought I had the subject mastered—I could add, subtract, multiply and divide with the best of them—torturous teachers cruelly introduced me to the "layers" of algebra, geometry, trigonometry and calculus. Actually "torture" is too nice a word to describe that process of discovery.

In the culinary world, the onion provides us with layer after layer of savory seasoning. Miners search for the strata of earth that hide the precious gems and metals they seek. I have no desire to revisit the different levels of math, but I love savoring a perfectly seasoned steak and enjoy the beauty of a sparkling diamond.

I also find it exciting and "delicious" when someone explores a familiar biblical truth, and seasons my life with another layer of its application and instruction. Jeremiah said, "Thy words were found, and I did eat them; and thy word was unto me the joy and rejoicing of my heart," (Jeremiah 15:16). Since God and His word are one, I'm sure we will never exhaust all of the Bible's riches. Someone told me recently they were informed by a rabbi that every Hebrew word (the language of scripture) has layer after layer of meanings—dozens of them. That would mean we'd better keep digging!

The excitement I experience from fresh revelation of God's word is precisely what Jacquie's book, *The Corporate Armor*, has produced in me. Though I have been fully expecting Holy Spirit to shine more light on the five anointings of Christ in Ephesians 4:11 (Apostle, Prophet, Evangelist, Pastor, and Teacher), I am nonetheless thrilled to see it happening. We must mature in our understanding of these gifts to the church, and we are.

Jacquie's revelation that these five functions and benefits are linked with our spiritual armor—and provide corporate armor—is beyond fascinating; it is profound. Read it. Peel off another layer and throw it in the stew. It'll taste better!

As a young boy, I was always fascinated by the unique accents, expressions and idioms of America's different regions. Unlike some, I never thought of the statements, many of which are grammatically incorrect, as being ignorant or inappropriate. I saw them as interesting, humorous and, at times, clever ways of expressing a region's individuality and style. In the same way, I don't see the tension in the five gifts of Ephesians 4:11 as competitive, nor one emphasis as being right and the others wrong. I see these anointings as different flavors of Christ, all of them important if we are to manifest the sweet savor of His knowledge to the world (2 Corinthians 2:14-15). We, the body of Christ, must be seasoned by all of them.

One of the humorous colloquialisms I heard as a kid that has stuck with me over the years was spoken by a hard-working, salt-of-the-earth man from the hills of Kentucky. He had invited my family to join his for a meal. Anyone familiar with Kentucky knows they have their own version of the English language! I've always loved the color and flavor it provides, even if at times I need an interpreter! This hard-working, generous man, after giving thanks for the food, looked at those of us around the table and said, "Dig in and go to takin' out."

And we ate. I mean, we ate! What a feast!

Though Jacquie has "proper" grammar—to her utter shame—the phrase is still appropriate for this feast of words: Dig in and go to takin' out!

I promise *ya'll*, you'll want seconds.

INTRODUCTION

QUITE SOME TIME AGO, while on a flight across the Pacific Ocean heading to Hawaii with my husband for some vacation time, I suddenly heard the Lord say, "I want to talk with you about the armor of God." Needless to say, I was not thinking about armor or warfare or any such thing. I was dreaming of tropical breezes, beautiful sights, fragrant flowers, waves crashing on shore, delicious food, and the gift of time together that we were about to enjoy.

What I heard next from Holy Spirit was something I had never thought or heard anyone else say. Very simply, I heard the Lord ask, "Since the letter to the Ephesians is a corporate book to the church in Ephesus, why is the armor always taught as for individuals? Should it not be understood for the corporate body as well?"

Now that got my attention.

For decades the Lord has focused much of my attention on the corporate aspects of the church, starting far before I understood ekklesia. I could see facets of God's intention of His sons and daughters being united in faith, purpose, and function. It was often frustrating to go into corporate prayer times and realize that for the most part, people were simply bringing their personal prayer time into the assembly without any connection with others in the room. And often they were not even listening to what was being prayed so that they might come into agreement. Through our place as sons and daughters of God, we become members one with another according to 1 Corinthians 12:12-13 and Ephesians 4:16. Each part is vitally important, supplying what is needed to cause the growth of the whole. What if we learned how to operate together, honoring and preferring one another in love, rightly discerning the body of Christ and recognizing the gifts, anointing, and callings of all the members of His body? What if we were corporately armored with the armor of God? What if...?

For the last several years, I have meditated, prayed, studied, researched, inquired, pondered, and waited to get clear direction and confirmation that this was a valid and needful revelation. Perhaps the delay has been my own insecurities that needed to be overcome, or perhaps it is simply that now is the time that we, as the body of Christ, need it. I won't even attempt to answer all those questions here, but I will proceed to share with you the revelation, understanding, and some application of what the Lord spoke to me that day 35,000 feet above sea level on my way to a vacation in paradise (a.k.a., Hawaii).

One more testimony: The first time I taught this in our local kingdom center, something amazing happened. The corporate armor was activated and we moved into a new place of enjoying the corporate protection of the Lord as a body and as individuals. I'll explain more on that later, but suffice it to say, that convinced me that now

Introduction

is the time for us to move forward in understanding The Corporate Armor.

I am convinced that as we learn to move together as His ekklesia, properly aligned and functioning according to His order and in obedience to the assignments of the Lord, we will be empowered to advance and be protected and victorious beyond anything we have seen.

Section 1

God's Armor of Protection

1 THE ARMOR OF GOD

Finally, be strong in the Lord and in the strength of His might. Put on the full armor of God, so that you will be able to stand firm against the schemes of the devil. For our struggle is not against flesh and blood, but against the rulers, against the powers, against the world forces of this darkness, against the spiritual forces of wickedness in the heavenly places. Therefore, take up the full armor of God, so that you will be able to resist in the evil day, and having done everything, to stand firm. Stand firm therefore, having girded your loins with truth, and having put on the breastplate of righteousness, and having shod your feet with the preparation of the gospel of peace; in addition to all, taking up the shield of faith with which you will be able to extinguish all the flaming arrows of the evil one. And take the helmet of salvation, and the sword of the Spirit, which is the word of God. With all prayer and petition pray at all times in the Spirit, and with this in view, be on the alert with all perseverance and petition for all the saints.

Ephesians 6:10-18

MOST OF US HAVE READ THIS PASSAGE and put on the armor of God regularly, if not daily, as a part of our devotional lives. We understand that the armor of God is given to us for protection against the diabolical schemes of the enemy that are set against us as the people of God. We take comfort in being protected by this mysterious armor and have sensed divine empowerment to go forth boldly in spiritual warfare, knowing God is protecting us by His very armor.

Likewise, we have been taught and recognize the armor as being Christ Himself. Jesus is our armor. He is the belt of truth, the breastplate of righteousness, the shoes of the preparation of the gospel of peace, the shield of faith, and the helmet of salvation as a covering of defense against the enemy; and His Word is the sword of the spirit that we take up offensively against the enemy.

This is good and it is right…but is that all?

AN INDIVIDUAL OR CORPORATE MESSAGE?

Paul, writing to the church in Ephesus, closes out his epistle to the Ephesians by giving some final instructions on how to stand victoriously in the ensuing battle against the adversary. To understand the context of the ending, we need to look back to the beginning. In the beginning, Paul addressed the church in Ephesus; it was plural, or corporate in nature, frequently including himself in the oratory using pronouns such as *us* and *we*. When he used the pronoun for *you*, it might actually be best translated in the southern vernacular of "y'all." While there is certainly nothing wrong in understanding and receiving these promises individually—in fact, the personal understanding enables us to fully embrace these truths on a broader corporate scale—that does not fully represent what Paul was writing.

Paul begins by reminding the Ephesian believers of their place of security within the family of God as sons of the Most High God by redemption that was secured in Christ (Ephesians 1:4-6). He encourages them by writing of the position they have as being seated in heavenly places with Christ "far above all rule and authority and power and dominion, and every name that is named, not only in this age but also in the one to come" (Ephesians 1:21). He speaks of them being "made alive together with Christ...and raised us up with Him, and seated us with Him in the heavenly places in Christ Jesus" (Ephesians 2:5-6). He goes on to talk about how in Christ both Jew and Gentile were made "into one" and made "the two into one new man." It all carries a context of addressing our place as a part of a corporate whole—Christ's body, the church, knit together and connected to the head, Christ Himself (Ephesians 4:14-16).

Building up to the text on the armor, everything Paul writes is in the context of the corporate unit known as the church—the ekklesia. This was not simply speaking to a single local congregation, but to the regional ekklesia made up of multiple smaller communities of believers. Today, some of these might be identified as congregations, house churches, or cell groups. Again, while these truths apply to the smaller unit—individual or community—ultimately Paul's address was to the corporate expression of the church—the regional ekklesia.

Most agree that the book of Ephesians is perhaps the crown jewel of Paul's writings and the one that provides some of the most valuable insights into church life. He addresses our positional standing (seated in heavenly places), our citizenships (ref. Ephesians 2:17-19), our structural stability (ref. Ephesians 2:20-22), our purpose (ref. Ephesians 3), our functional alignments (ref. Ephesians 4), our relational connectivity (ref. Ephesians 5) and finally, our military armor (ref. Ephesians 6).

Given that the purpose of this book is the armor of God, let's take a few minutes to briefly review the pieces of the armor and the protection each provides.

COMPONENTS OF THE ARMOR OF GOD

BELT OF TRUTH

First, we are instructed to "gird your loins with truth." Other translations say, "put on the belt of truth." This piece of armor fits around the body much like a girdle, surrounding the loins with security. The loin area of the body speaks of reproduction and progeny. Truth protects the future hope of the church. Truth guards against the infiltration of anything that would cause error or compromise to come into the ongoing life of the body. Truth serves to secure the foundation of the body. It is the first piece of armor to be put on, and interestingly, in Roman times, the soldier's belt was crucial to his overall preparedness for battle. The Roman soldier's belt was very wide and served to hold a lot of equipment: a loop for different swords, other loops for ropes, darts, and a ration sack. When they went into battle to conquer a city, the soldiers would empty their ration sacks to make room for the spoils of battle—the gold, jewelry and other valuables that were available after the conquest. The belt was securely tied in several places so it would stay in place. No matter how the soldier moved, the belt was secure with the tools of warfare needed for the situation at hand. If the belt was not on properly, then all that was attached to the belt for his use would be out of place, presenting a decrease of efficiency and effectiveness in the midst of battle. It could even cost him his life. This is quite a picture of the integral function of the belt of truth as being foundational, protective over our lives and that of future generations, and of how it is integrated into the proper function and strength of the rest of the armor.

BREASTPLATE OF RIGHTEOUSNESS

Secondly, it is the "breastplate of righteousness" that is emphasized as crucially important. The area of protection is that of the vital organs of life—primarily the heart, which is of utmost importance to life and the pumping of the blood to distribute the breath of life into all of the body. Righteousness is a key protection against the entrance of the enemy that always seeks to kill and steal the breath of life from God's people. Righteousness guards the heart against evil and secures what is released by the breath of the lungs as spoken words flowing from the heart that will not defile but will produce life.

Righteousness is not simply about right-standing before the Lord, but also about right-living as a demonstration of Christ's life to the world. It is a protection of our life and destiny and a protection of the heart of our confession that Jesus Christ is the son of the living God who fully defeated Satan by living free of sin.

The breastplate of righteousness is closely connected to the belt of truth. Again, using the Roman soldier's armor as a visual picture, the breastplate was literally connected to the belt, which was put on first to provide a secure foundation for the breastplate. It is imperative that righteousness be linked with truth to provide a solid foundation for the life of soldiers serving in the Army of the Lord.

In Psalm 15 (NKJV), the Psalmist prays, "Lord, who may abide in Your tabernacle? Who may dwell in Your holy hill? He who walks uprightly, and works righteousness, and speaks the truth in his heart." Then, in Zechariah 8:8, God declares of Himself concerning His people who had been taken captive, "I will bring them back and they will live in the midst of Jerusalem; and they shall be My people, and I will be their God in truth and righteousness." So, even in the armor, truth and righteousness are foundational to the reality of the Lord's nature and our entrance into His presence.

SHOES OF THE PREPARATION OF THE GOSPEL OF PEACE

Thirdly, the feet are shod with the "preparation of the gospel of peace." This portion of the armor protects against the treacherous obstacles, snares, and traps that are set in the world. The footwear of the Roman soldier had spikes on the soles, providing them a strong stance and balance that secured them into a superior posture in battle regardless of the terrain where they were engaged in battle. Likewise, the shoes protect as we go out into the world, providing stability, strength, and security to trample on serpents, scorpions and every evil thing, bringing the enemy under the crushing weight of the gospel of peace.

These shoes, unlike shoes of leather, are the byproduct of the gospel of peace. Romans 16:20 declares, "The God of peace will soon crush Satan under your feet." It is the peace of God that passes all understanding that enables us to advance the kingdom into the world against all natural odds. As we are prepared by the gospel of peace working in us and through us, we are enabled to go out and trample the enemy and have no harm come to us.

The "shoes of the preparation of the gospel of peace" empower us to become peacemakers, not just peacekeepers, through bringing the light of the gospel into situations to resolve conflict and bring order out of disorder. They prepare and protect the body and provide confidence to go out and reach beyond the safety of our own fellowship of believers and our preferred comfort zones.

SHIELD OF FAITH

Fourthly, we are instructed to lift up the shield of faith by which we are able to extinguish the fiery darts of the evil one. We know the enemy is always shooting off darts in hope of penetrating through our weak and vulnerable places to bring harm or even death. The shield of faith provides a sure defense against the lies of the enemy. Faith, rooted in truth, established in righteousness and lived out in peace, puts out the enemy's accusations and taunts of defeat and demise. Faith is a gift that we must "take up" or activate—put into action. It is not something we simply wear but something that requires engagement.

The Roman shield was long, rectangular, and covered the knees-to-chin to protect against arrows and spears. It could be knelt behind during an arrow barrage. One interesting aspect of the Roman soldier's shield was its ability for groups of soldiers to come together in a military formation called "phalanx." This strategy allowed soldiers to join in close proximity to each other in order to create a tight circle to protect the larger group from the influx of fiery darts.

Faith believes and acts based on the Word of God, and moves out in trust in the truth of what God has said. The shield of faith is the portion of the armor that is out in front, and in major battles, linked up with other shields to put up a wall of defense against enemy attacks.

There is an aspect of the shield of faith that does not simply cause the enemy's arrows to bounce off. It extinguishes the fire of the enemy's attacks. Faith douses fear. Faith calms agitation. Faith comforts the fainthearted. Faith strengthens the resolve of the attacked and strips the attacker of his power. Faith ensures victory for those trusting in the Lord as their strong tower and sure defense.

HELMET OF SALVATION

Our fifth piece of armor is the helmet of salvation given to protect the head, representing our mind and way of thinking. One of the key means the enemy seeks to hold believers captive is through belief systems, mindsets, and patterns of thought that do not agree with truth. He also seeks to introduce teachings and systems of belief that are contrary to the Word of God. The enemy is persistent in speaking lies and accusations to keep God's people in captivity and bondage and to stop forward movement. The helmet of salvation, like the other pieces of the armor, is vitally important. Interestingly enough, in our use of Roman armor as our visual, the ancient Roman helmet was the most advanced of its time, far superior to that of other nations. The design provided leather insides for better fit and comfort, a chin strap to hold in place, and a visor to protect the eyes. Its shape extended down to protect the sides and back of the neck, and the exterior was made of various metals depending upon the rank of service within the army.

The helmet of salvation is instrumental in ensuring that our thoughts line up with the reality of salvation. Romans 12:2 instructs us, "Do not be conformed to this world, but be transformed by the renewing of your mind." In other words, our thinking has to be renewed. It has to catch up with the spiritual truths of our salvation. If our thinking does not agree with spiritual truth, we will simply continue to live a limited measure of the salvation that Christ has purchased for us. It does not make our salvation any less authentic, but it does make it less real and effective in our daily experience of the abundant life, and it limits our ability to move out in the fullness of trust and obedience to what God has purposed for us to walk in.

Corporately, the helmet of salvation is a guard for the church to remain true to the fullness of our salvation in Christ. Our salvation is not only what we are saved *from*, but also what we are saved *unto*—all that Christ purposed for us as His ekklesia; His church, living in community as family and in authority to advance His kingdom on earth as it is in heaven. The helmet guards our minds against the subtle and sometimes not-so-subtle attacks of the enemy sent to erode and even pervert the truths of scripture. We desperately need the helmet of salvation.

SWORD OF THE SPIRIT

The Word of God is our sword of the spirit and we take it up as a weapon against the enemy to defeat and overcome every onslaught. The sword of the spirit is both defensive and offensive. We wield it against the enemy's attacks and we use it to cut through the obstacles and lines of opposition that are set before us. Using Holy Spirit-breathed Word as a weapon against the enemy is powerfully accurate and effective to defeat every attack of the enemy.

The Roman sword that Paul is referring to here is the two-edged sword that was able to cut in both directions, inflict a mortal blow, and even rip the enemy's insides to shreds. This points out to us that a Word from the Lord, strategically released out of our mouths like a sword, is capable of wielding a death blow that utterly dismembers the hidden mechanisms of the enemy's schemes that are at work.

The sword of the spirit becomes a force of the vengeance of the Lord when we pick it up to use, fully armored in truth, righteousness, peace, faith, and salvation. When the sword is used without these foundational and protective portions of the Lord's character and authority in place, we can find ourselves vulnerable to the schemes of the enemy.

PRAYING ALWAYS

While prayer may not be pictured as a physical piece of armor, it is nonetheless vitally important. Without praying always, we might presume to move without direction from our Commander-in-Chief. By prayer, we are properly postured in submission to the Lord to obey His commands and His alone. James 4:7 makes this plain as it is written, "Submit therefore to God. Resist the devil and he will flee from you." By prayer, the soldier knows his assignment, his position, and his timing as revealed through prayer.

Prayer is the communication line that links heaven and earth and brings the Army of the Lord on the earth into alignment with the assignments of heaven. When we come into proper alignment with the assignments of the Lord, our mouths are filled with declarations and decrees of kingly intercession to pray the purposes of the Commander-in-Chief, the King of kings and Lord of lords. As these words are released out of our mouths, the angelic Armies of Heaven respond to battle on our behalf—for us and with us against the forces of the enemy.

Again, going back to the original question I heard Holy Spirit ask me, "Since the letter to the Ephesians is a corporate book to the church in Ephesus, why is the armor always taught as for individuals? Should it not be understood for the corporate body as well?"

Questions for Your Consideration

I. How have you experienced the protection of the armor of God in your own life?
II. Consider where you need to be personally strengthened in the various aspects of the armor.
III. How are you growing in unity with the armor of God and all its attributes?

A Prayer for You to Pray

Father God,

Thank You for providing us with Your armor to protect and shield us as we walk through life facing the schemes of the enemy who is consistently waging war against us and our pursuit of living fully for You. Teach us, Lord, how to grow into greater and greater union with Your armor; walking in truth, righteousness, peace, faith, the fullness of salvation, wielding the sharp two-edged sword of Your Word as we engage in all manner of prayer to see Your kingdom come and Your will done on earth as it is in heaven. In Jesus' name.

Amen.

2 The Church Jesus Is Building

Now when Jesus came into the district of Caesarea Philippi, He was asking His disciples, "Who do people say that the Son of Man is?"

And they said, "Some say John the Baptist; and others, Elijah; but still others, Jeremiah, or one of the prophets."

He said to them, "But who do you say that I am?"

Simon Peter answered, "You are the Christ, the Son of the living God."

And Jesus said to him, 'Blessed are you, Simon Barjona, because flesh and blood did not reveal this to you, but My Father who is in heaven.

'I also say to you that you are Peter, and upon this rock I will build My church; and the gates of Hades will not overpower it.'

"I will give you the keys of the kingdom of heaven; and whatever you bind on earth shall have been bound in heaven, and whatever you loose on earth shall have been loosed in heaven."

Then He warned the disciples that they should tell no one that He was the Christ.

Matthew 16:13-20

WHEN JESUS STOOD AT CAESAREA PHILIPPI declaring to His disciples, "upon this rock I will build My church; and the gates of Hades will not overpower it" (Matthew 16:18), He was providing key insights into our purpose and destiny. We must understand the word Jesus used for *church* if we are going to grasp the fullness of what He was communicating. The word Jesus chose to use was *ekklesia,* which generally speaks of the assembly of saints, but within the cultural context of the understanding of the times, the disciples would have recognized it as a governmental word, not a religious word. I am not attempting to provide an extensive treatment of the word *ekklesia* here, only to share an overview. There are others who are far more capable to expound on this important topic.

Ekklesia spoke of the corporate assembly of delegates set in place to legislate and govern according to the kingdom they represent. In other words, Jesus was saying that upon the rock of revelation that He was the Son of God, He was going to build an assembly of delegates, ambassadors, to legislate and govern on earth according to the will of God and the culture of the kingdom of God. He was speaking of the corporate expression of His government being established on earth that would be powerfully victorious against the onslaughts of the enemy and would effectively bring about the ever-increasing reality of His "kingdom come on earth as it is in heaven" (Matthew 6:10).

I find it interesting that Jesus chose this location at Caesarea Philippi in front of the Temple Pan, which opened to what was referred to as the "gate of hell," to bring forth this revelation. Jesus chose the place where the enemy had established a formidable presence, to declare that what He was building, nothing could defeat, not even this place of hellish worship, sacrifices and evil. Powerful!

From the beginning, Jesus was speaking of the corporate nature of His church. The ekklesia was to be the coming together of many members into an assembly to function as one body. It was not just a gathering of people; it was the assembling of many parts for the purpose of function. Years ago, the Lord spoke to me about the difference between gathering and assembly by saying you can gather all the parts to a bicycle but until they are assembled, the bicycle cannot function and fulfill the purpose for which it was created. It is time for the church to move from simply gathering, to being assembled for the purpose of function.

The Apostle Paul brings even more perspective to the corporate nature of the church through the analogies of being a family, a temple and a body. We also can clearly see that we are also enlisted as soldiers in the Army of the Lord in 2 Timothy and that we are to be, and will be, engaged in warfare against spiritual forces of darkness, as seen in 2 Corinthians 10:4 and Ephesians 6:12. Let's consider for a moment the temple and the body to see the corporate nature of what God has purposed and revealed in these metaphors.

The Church as the Family of God

So, you are not foreigners or guests, but rather you are the children of the city of the holy ones, with all the rights as family members of the household of God.

Ephesians 2:19 TPT

From the very beginning of creation, God was looking for a family to occupy, subdue, and manifest His kingdom on earth as it is in heaven. From Adam and Eve, God set in motion His purpose, but through the fall, that purpose had to be redeemed through Christ. The purposes of God are being progressively restored through those who would place their trust in Christ and become members of the royal family of God as heirs and joint-heirs with Jesus the Christ, His church.

While most, if not all of us to some degree, only know family from a perspective of varying measures of dysfunction, God desires and has paid the price for healing and restoration so that we might be made one family who love, live, and function together in ways that will produce growth, maturity, and multiplication according to God's original design.

In a recent celebration at CityGate Atlanta—the kingdom center that I lead—several people shared testimonies of what it has meant to be a part of CityGate Atlanta; not just functioning as the ekklesia but as family. One after another talked about how they had been loved, cared for, helped, and strengthened in various ways in their personal journey. Then, each one connected the family aspect to how it helped them to grow and mature so they could more effectively function within the ekklesia. You see, being connected as family, caring for one another, sharing life together in good times and in the challenging times, fortifies, strengthens, challenges, and becomes the place of healing and restoration.

What a blessing to be a part of the marvelous and mysterious family of God!

THE CHURCH AS THE TEMPLE OF THE LORD

Now, therefore, you are no longer strangers and foreigners, but fellow citizens with the saints and members of the household of God, having been built on the foundation of the apostles and prophets, Jesus Christ Himself being the chief cornerstone, in whom the whole building, being fitted together, grows into a holy temple in the Lord, in whom you also are being built together for a dwelling place of God in the Spirit.

Ephesians 2:19-22 NKJV

You are rising like the perfectly fitted stones of the temple; and your lives are being built up together upon the ideal foundation laid by the apostles and prophets, and best of all, you are connected to the Head Cornerstone of the building, the Anointed One, Jesus Christ himself! This entire building is under construction and is continually growing under his supervision until it rises up completed as the holy temple of the Lord himself. This means that God is transforming each one of you into the Holy of Holies, his dwelling place, through the power of the Holy Spirit living in you!

Ephesians 2:20-22 TPT

> *For we are God's fellow workers; you are God's field, you are God's building. Do you not know that you are the temple of God and that the Spirit of God dwells in you?*
>
> 1 Corinthians 3:9 & 16 NKJV

In the Old Covenant, Solomon built a temple made of stones. The stones used in Solomon's temple were quarried and chiseled to fit together precisely. These stones were positioned according to the design as a beautifully glorious dwelling place of God. There was nothing else like it, and when the priests came together in one accord to worship in the dedication of the temple, the glory of the Lord so filled the temple that no flesh could stand! (See 2 Chronicles 5-7) What an amazing foreshadowing of what God intends His temple made of living stones to be like!

Under the New Covenant, through Christ, we are being fit together into the living temple of the Lord, the place of dwelling of the Lord. God's plan from the beginning was to have a place that extended the reality of His kingdom into the earth, as a dwelling place of God, a temple not made out of bricks and mortar but of living stones that fit together according to His design and purpose for the display of His splendor, and as a place where His governmental authority would be established.

This living temple of God is not centralized or limited to a singular geographical location. Rather, it functions according to the assignments of the King within the boundaries that He establishes to bring kingdom domain into communities, cities, regions, and nations. A temple in the spirit, made up of redeemed humanity being properly fit together with each part doing its part, brings ever-increasing measures of the manifest presence and domain of the Lord into the earth.

The church as the temple of the Lord clearly indicates the corporate nature of our union with Christ and with those who have surrendered their lives to Christ's redeeming grace, those who are submitted to the fashioning and shaping to fulfill the place and purpose that the Lord Himself has chosen. Each living stone is unique and valuable, but it cannot fulfill its ultimate purpose apart from being properly fit into the corporate building of the temple of the Lord.

The temple made of living stones is truly a sign and a wonder on the earth. I'm sure that you, too, have been in worship gatherings where the pieces all come together, the living stones are caught up together in exalting the Lord, creating a place of His habitation. The glory is tangible as each one connects with those around them without regard to division, worshiping and praising the Lord. Holy Spirit, who dwells in each one, suddenly and marvelously fills the temple. There are no words to describe the wonder of those moments!

While, at this time, we may see these moments as rare, I am convinced this is what God not only desires to do but is beginning to do throughout the earth as He brings us into a greater and greater understanding and reality of being built up together into His holy temple. Let all the saints cry, "GLORY!"

THE CHURCH AS THE BODY OF CHRIST

For just as we have many members in one body and all the members do not have the same function, so we, who are many, are one body in Christ, and individually members one of another.

Romans 12:4-5

For even as the body is one and yet has many members, and all the members of the body, though they are many, are one body, so also is Christ.

1 Corinthians 12:12

And He put all things in subjection under His feet, and gave Him as head over all things to the church, which is His body, the fullness of Him who fills all in all.

Ephesians 1:22-23

Here's the secret: The gospel of grace has made you, non-Jewish believers, into coheirs of his promise through your union with him. And you have now become members of His body—one with the Anointed One!

Ephesians 3:6 TPT

Christ has one body, one church, and we are each individual members of the corporate body of Christ. Individually, we are "in Christ" but individually we are not the "body of Christ." We are part of the whole, but we are not the whole. This seems so simple that you may wonder why I waste time stating the obvious. However, in our western culture, let me ask this question: How often have you heard individuals say, "I am the church"? I am certain you have and perhaps have even said it yourself. I certainly have. (No condemnation, just a reality check for all of us!)

Unfortunately, we have allowed our independent mindsets to so infiltrate our belief systems that we proclaim things as truth that are not true. We rarely recognize the error we are proclaiming. It sounds good. It has an element of truth in it, but it is not the whole truth. We must line up with God's truth...and nothing but the truth!

In 1 Corinthians 12, the Apostle Paul clearly reveals the mystery of us all being set into the body of Christ as many parts of the whole, just as it is in the human body. In the human body, each part is vital, each part has a function, each part is to be honored, protected, and used according to its purpose. So it is in the body of Christ. Body parts out of place, missing, or not properly functioning cause limitations to the body functioning at maximum potential and can cause the body to not be able to function beyond the bare minimum to sustain life. This can lead to death.

Jesus is the head, and He only has one body. His body is made up of many parts, and each part is vitally important. The individual parts are valuable and treasured, but as we often say, we are better and stronger together than we are apart! We need each other.

The body of Christ doesn't just need all of the parts present, it needs each and every member rightly connected and aligned for the optimum purpose of its function. When one part of the body is weak, injured, or disengaged, the whole is weakened.

Several years ago, while bounding down the steps of my home in a bigger rush than was wise, I learned just how limited the body can become when just one part is injured! On this fateful day, I completely missed the bottom step and suddenly found myself sprawled out on the foyer floor with my left foot no longer in the position it was created to be in. While it wasn't a particularly bad break, it most definitely hurt (bad!) and significantly hindered my ability to get around and do the things I needed to do! It also caused other parts of my body to suffer and be forced to compensate for the lack of use of my left leg.

As the body of Christ, it seems we are often limping around with a broken ankle. Or perhaps it is a hand that is injured, eyes that can't see, ears that can't hear…or perhaps the parts are present but not properly functioning and doing what they were created to do. Just like your body needs all its parts functioning and healthy, so does the body of Christ.

In our modern culture, we have become far too independent and self-sufficient, and as a result, find ourselves weakened and easily defeated, even viewed as a dead religious organization rather than a dynamic spiritual life-giving body. The strain on the body of Christ caused by a lack of understanding and submission to the purpose, placement, and function that God created each part to fill has wreaked havoc on the strength, vitality, and mission of the body of Christ. Paul says it this way in 1 Corinthians 12:18-20: "But God has carefully designed each member and placed it in the body to function as he desires. Diversity is required, for if the body consisted of one single part, there wouldn't be a body at all! So now we see that there are many different parts and functions, but one body." (TPT)

Furthermore, vain imaginations, jealousy, competition, strife, rejection, accusations, and even dismemberment of members of the body have become pandemic, paralyzing and stymying the growth, multiplication, maturity, and proper function of the church. Galatians 5:15 warns us of the dangers we now see far too rampant in the church today: "But if you continue to criticize and come against each other over minor issues, you're acting like wild beasts trying to destroy one another!" (TPT)

THE CHURCH AS THE EKKLESIA, LEGISLATIVE ASSEMBLY OF THE KINGDOM ON EARTH

We started this chapter looking at Jesus' words in Matthew 16:18, saying that He would build His church, His ekklesia, and the gates of hell would not prevail against it. I want to close this chapter coming full circle so that we see that all of these expressions of the church—His temple, His family, His body, and His ekklesia—reveal to us the mysterious ways of the Lord to bring His kingdom on earth as it is in heaven. If we simply focus on any one of these facets without seeing how they fit together and bring strength to the fullness of God's purposes, we may accomplish much and enjoy unique expressions of our union with Christ. But what if we came into a greater measure of the whole? What would that look like? What impact in the world could we have?

God's intended purpose was for us to be fit together according to His purposes as one temple, one glorious royal family of the King of kings and Lord of lords, one body of our Lord Jesus Christ and His ekklesia to bring the rule and culture of the kingdom of God into the earth.

Can you imagine what could be accomplished in bringing more of Christ's kingdom on earth if we truly lived in accordance with His marvelous design?

THE CHURCH TOGETHER FULFILLING DESTINY

Paul, in Ephesians 2:10, as translated in The Passion Translation (TPT), writes of the church:

We have become His poetry, a recreated people that will fulfill the destiny He has given each of us, for we are joined to Jesus, the Anointed One. Even before we were born, God planned, in advance, our destiny and the good works we would do to fulfill it!

In other words, as we allow the Lord to fashion and fit us together, we become a magnificent poem for others to read, so that according to Ephesians 3:10 "the manifold wisdom of God might now be made known through the church to the rulers and the authorities in the heavenly places." God has ordained that the only way the ultimate fullness of destiny can be reached is through the church, the corporate man, moving together in oneness of purpose with each part doing its part.

It is a mystery to our human mind that we could be so knit together through and in Christ that we truly become one, members one with another, operating and functioning without division, strife or contention, being strengthened as each joint supplies, and protected as we are armored together with the very armor of God.

Now that we clearly see the corporate nature of the church, let's take a look at the armor of God from a perspective of the church being one body made up of many members.

Questions for Your Consideration

I. What description of the church do you most relate to? Which expression have you most often experienced through being a part of the church?

II. Which description do you believe that you personally need to grow in understanding and expression of in order to more fully function as a part of what Christ is building as His church—His body, family temple, army or ekklesia?

III. How do you see that increased understanding and experience of the corporate nature of the church can help us more completely fulfill the mission of Christ and His kingdom through the church?

A Prayer for You to Pray

Heavenly Father,

I thank You for the revelation of Your Word and the amazing ways Your Word speaks to us about our union with Christ and each other. Forgive me for the ways I have looked at my place in Your church from an individualistic perspective and have missed the blessings of being rightly connected to others that You have made abundantly clear in Your Word. Help me, Lord, to see and embrace with greater clarity the reality of functioning together as members of Your body fitly joined together with every joint supplying what is needed; bringing the grace that You have given to each one to benefit the whole; serving together under Your headship to see Your kingdom purposes advanced on the earth as it is in heaven. Teach me, Lord, how to live authentically as

Yours with all the saints so that together we might bring You glory and honor. In Jesus' matchless name.

Amen.

3 United and Protected

Stand firm therefore, having girded your loins with truth, and having put on the breastplate of righteousness, and having shod your feet with the preparation of the gospel of peace; in addition to all, taking up the shield of faith with which you will be able to extinguish all the flaming arrows of the evil one. And take the helmet of salvation, and the sword of the Spirit, which is the word of God.

Ephesians 6:14-17

As we have seen, God has ordained that we function corporately as His body. Ephesians 4:15-16 states that we are to "grow up in all aspects into Him who is the head, even Christ, from whom the whole body, being fitted and held together by what every joint supplies, according to the proper working of each individual part, causes the growth of the body for the building up of itself in love." When every part of a body is properly functioning, the body is strong and can accomplish amazing things, both in the natural and in the spiritual.

If we are one body and we are in a spiritual war, then we need corporate armor to face the diabolical attacks that are coming against the church. We need personal armor to be protected against personal battles, but there are battles over territories that require the church to rise up together to fight. In territorial battles, it isn't the individual soldier that will win the battle, it is the corporate ekklesia coming together in oneness of purpose to do the bidding of our Commander in Chief. In these battles, as stated in Ephesians 6, the fight is "against the rulers, against the powers, against the world forces of this darkness, against the spiritual forces of wickedness in the heavenly places." It is a spiritually cosmic battle, one where the church contends together as a strong, well-trained, positioned-for-victory fighting machine!

PROTECTED TOGETHER

We can see the foreshadowing of this in the Old Testament in various contexts. One of my favorites is found in First Chronicles 12:23-40. Here we see the divisions of the tribes of Israel gathering at Hebron to turn the kingdom of Saul over to David. These verses reveal the various and specific areas of expertise and function of the divisions of the army that came together for the purpose of serving and doing their part to see that the kingdom was firmly established under King David's rulership. This is a wonderful picture of God's purposes for the various parts found to make up the church in our day with each part doing its part for the good of God's kingdom.

The soldiers in the divisions of the Army of Israel were expertly equipped for war, and they knew how to move in rank and formation according to their assignment, position, and function within the army. As the army in David's day came together at Hebron and went out under his leadership with the assigned captains in place, there was strength and victory.

During the years of King David's reign, we see how the tribes came together, each bringing the best of who they were under the leadership of King David, with the appointed leaders to function in alignment with the purposes of the assignment at hand. When there were breaches in the ranks or betrayals among the leaders, trouble ensued because the armor was not fully secured. When they moved together in victory, it is clear to see that they knew how to stay in formation, move forward in rank, and win victory after victory by following the established order of the Lord in truth and righteousness. The children of Israel under King David were protected as he led them forth in truth, righteousness, peace, faith, and salvation.

Another favorite is found in 2 Chronicles 20 when Judah, under the leadership of King Jehoshaphat, is facing a confederation of enemy forces of Moab, Ammon, and Mount Seir (ref. 2 Chronicles 20:10) that could have certainly defeated them. The scriptures reveal that Jehoshaphat was afraid and set himself to seek the Lord, calling a fast throughout all Judah that together they might seek the Lord. Jehoshaphat prayed and all Judah stood before the Lord, waiting for the Lord's reply.

The prophet Jahaziel answered and revealed the Lord's instruction and strategy.

Be not afraid or dismayed at this great multitude, for the battle is not yours, but God's. Go down against them tomorrow. Behold, they will come up by the ascent of Ziz, and you will find them at the end of the river valley, in front of the Wilderness of Jeruel. You need not fight in this battle; take your positions, stand and witness the salvation of the Lord who is with you, O Judah and Jerusalem. Do not fear or be dismayed; tomorrow go out against them, for the Lord is with you.

2 Chronicles 20:15-17 NKJV

The words of the prophet brought the whole company of people into alignment with the purposes of the Lord. It also provided instruction on how to walk out the assignment (go up but you won't have to fight). They were given the position (stand) and posture (faith) they were to take. The prophetic instructions provided understanding of the intention of the Lord (salvation and victory), a challenge to guard their hearts (do not fear or be dismayed), and a command to advance (go out against them). Jehoshaphat bowed down before the Lord in worship, while the Levites, Kohathites, and some of the Korahites stood up to praise with a loud voice.

Jehoshaphat laid hold of the word, instructed the people saying, "Put your trust in the Lord your God and you will be established. Put your trust in His prophets and succeed." He then convened a council and gave strategic instructions to the people based upon the revelation and council received. In an act of displaying their absolute trust in the Lord and His Word, the King appointed the praisers to go out before the army singing, "Give thanks to the Lord, for His lovingkindness is everlasting" (2 Chronicles 20:21). In the natural, facing formidable foes, this instruction would seem ludicrous. But Jehoshaphat had a word from the Lord and had come to an understanding of how to implement the word in full assurance of faith.

As the children of Israel moved out with Judah leading the way, lifting up songs of exuberant praise, declaring the goodness and eternal mercy of the Lord, God sent out the ambushes against the enemy and completely routed them. The prophetic word, properly interpreted and strategically implemented, resulted in a victory that was exceedingly above what they could have imagined. What an amazing victory and one I am certain we all love to hear again and again!

My point in retelling this story is to emphasize the way God used King Jehoshaphat and the Prophet Jahaziel to bring the people of Judah into proper positioning so that every member is doing their part in accordance with the purposes of God. They went into battle armored, in a sense, by aligning with truth (what God says), righteousness (obeying what He says), peace (calm assurance of well-being found in the Lord), faith (trusting in the Lord without fear or doubting), and salvation (assured by the hand of the Lord). Can you see it? Truth, righteousness, peace, faith, and assurance of salvation formed a powerful armor for the Army of Judah against formidable foes.

As it was for the Children of Israel, how much more true is it for the ekklesia today?

TOGETHER PROTECTED IN CHRIST

As we move forward into the New Covenant through Christ, we see that Jesus is our Divine Protector. We are hidden with Christ in God according to Colossians 3:3.

Ephesians 1:20-23 states that He is seated at the right hand of God the Father, "far above all rule and authority and power and dominion, and every name that is named, not only in this age but also in the one to come. And He put all things in subjection under His feet, and gave Him as head over all things to the church, which is His body, the fullness of Him who fills all in all." Then, according to Ephesians 2:6, the Apostle Paul declares that He has "seated us with Him in the heavenly places in Christ Jesus."

Now, I would say that is a place of being protected!

I would also suggest that we need to come to a deeper place of maturity in our understanding of what it means to be protected. In modern culture, we tend to think of being protected as a condition of not ever facing difficulties, challenges, pain, suffering, loss, or any type of warfare. However, from a biblical perspective, that perspective does not line up. Jesus, the very Son of God, as well as the early apostles, suffered greatly through persecution, beatings, imprisonments, and death through some of the most horrific means known to man. Likewise, the early church, as well as many around the world today, live daily under dire persecution. So, I would propose that protection does not equal lack of trouble, warfare, or suffering, but rather a divine enablement of strength by God's grace to "having done everything, to stand firm" (Ephesians 6:13). It is the protection of spirit and soul to stand against the intrusions of lies and compromises to the gospel of the kingdom, the temptations to veer into unrighteousness of heart and lifestyle, the situations that would cause our feet to stumble or to rob us of the peace of God, the fiery darts that assault our faith, and the teachings and doctrines of demons that bombard the mind.

In fact, Romans 5:1-5 clearly gives us the kingdom perspective: "Therefore, having been justified by faith, we have peace with God through our Lord Jesus Christ, through whom also we have access by faith into this grace in which we stand, and rejoice in hope of the glory of God. And not only that, but we also glory in tribulations, knowing that tribulation produces perseverance; and perseverance, character; and character, hope. Now hope does not disappoint, because the love of God has been poured out in our hearts by the Holy Spirit who was given to us." It is only by God's grace that we can stand in the midst of trials and tribulations and He has provided everything we need!

The armor of God provides us with what is needed to stay true to Christ and His purposes—no matter what!

Most of us, if not all, have been taught and believe that the ultimate armor of God is Christ Himself as our protector. That is without question! Yet, as the Lord continued to speak to me somewhere over the Pacific Ocean, He began to reveal a mystery of how He has chosen to armor us as the corporate body. Could this be something we have missed…or at least I had? Very clearly Holy Spirit said, "Turn back from Ephesians 6 to Ephesians 4, I want to show you something." I had no idea what to expect, but still today I can sense the expectation that His words brought to my spirit.

I began to read, and when I came to Ephesians 4:11 where Paul writes, "And He [Christ] gave some as apostles, and some as prophets, and some as evangelists, and some as pastors and teachers," Holy Spirit said, "Stop and read it again." As I did, I pondered the initial question the Lord had asked me: "Since the letter to the Ephesians is a corporate book to the church in Ephesus, why is the armor always taught as for individuals? Should it not be understood for the corporate body as well?"

As I did, I suddenly saw it. The five-fold giftings given to the church perfectly overlay the function of each piece of the armor of God in the order written.

I sat and stared at the pages of my Bible wondering, could this really be true?

Questions for Your Consideration

I. How do you spiritually and practically "put on the armor" of God?

II. Think of ways you have seen the armor of God active in your life. How did you experience the protection of the armor of God: truth, righteousness, peace, faith, and salvation?

III. Have you ever felt unprotected or that you were not properly armored for the battles you were facing?

IV. Consider times when you may have felt you were all alone in a time of intense battle. How did you make it through those times? What did you yearn for in the most intense times?

A Prayer for You to Pray

Lord,

Thank You for being our security, protector, defender, and guard. You are the shield about me, my stronghold, and the place where I find refuge. And, I thank You that You have provided Your armor of truth, righteousness, peace, faith, and salvation for us to put on and use through all the battles we face in this life. Today, with renewed faith in all that You have provided, I put on the full armor of God and ask that You would enable me, by Your grace, to embrace and engage with the protection and the weapons of Your Word and prayer to advance in victory for Your name's sake.

Amen.

4 Armored by Christ's Leadership Anointings

And He gave some as apostles, and some as prophets, and some as evangelists, and some as pastors and teachers, for the equipping of the saints for the work of service, to the building up of the body of Christ; until we all attain to the unity of the faith, and of the knowledge of the Son of God, to a mature man, to the measure of the stature which belongs to the fullness of Christ. As a result, we are no longer to be children, tossed here and there by waves and carried about by every wind of doctrine, by the trickery of men, by craftiness in deceitful scheming; but speaking the truth in love, we are to grow up in all aspects into Him who is the head, even Christ, from whom the whole body, being fitted and held together by what every joint supplies, according to the proper working of each individual part, causes the growth of the body for the building up of itself in love.

Ephesians 4:11-16

Before we proceed, we need to establish a basic understanding of the five-fold grace-gifts (as they are often referred) that are listed in Ephesians 4:11. They are the five expressions of Christ's divine leadership that He gives to operate through men and women designated to provide leadership to the church. Those whom Christ has called, He empowers to provide guidance, instruction, equipping, discipleship, and protection as His representatives. The persons called to these functions of leadership are gifts of Christ and are able to fulfill the function only according to the grace that Christ alone gives.

To glean some perspective, we can look at the life of Jesus when He walked on the earth. We see the ways He functioned and observe the protection that operated as a type of armor around His followers, particularly the twelve disciples.

Jesus, as apostle, was constantly establishing kingdom truth. He came preaching and demonstrating the kingdom of God. He worked with His disciples to lead them into maturity to fulfill their purposes through teaching, sharing life together, and allowing them to face opportunities, obstacles, and tests to strengthen their internal resolve to follow the way of the Lord, no matter what. He was securing truth as a firm foundation into the very core of their beings to protect them against the battles they would face in the days ahead. He prepared them to be sent into their purposes with strength of spirit that would not fail, even though it was tested severely at times. In the end, they would finish the work they were created to do (ref. Matthew 16).

Jesus, as prophet, established the standard of righteousness that was not merely external to be seen by man, but was revealed in the deepest thoughts and intents of the heart. He confronted hypocrisy, double standards, and religiosity that would never stand the test of true holiness. As prophet, Jesus pointed the way to living with clean hands, a pure heart, not operating in falsehood, or swearing deceitfully (ref. Psalm 24) so that the enemy would have no place of effective access against them (ref. Matthew 23). When He saw unrighteousness, He confronted it and pointed the way of escape to the paths of righteousness (ref. Matthew 15:10-12, Luke 3:7-9 as examples).

Jesus, as evangelist, equipped His followers to go out into all the world to make disciples, to not fear what could harm them from the outside, but to go and trample on serpents, scorpions, and every evil thing in order to take the power of the gospel of the kingdom to those in desperate need of a Savior. We see this in Luke 10:2-3 when Jesus sent the 70 out: "The harvest is plentiful, but the laborers are few; therefore beseech the Lord of the harvest to send out laborers into His harvest. Go; behold, I send you out as lambs in the midst of wolves."

Then, in verse 19, He said to them: "Behold, I have given you authority to tread on serpents and scorpions, and over all the power of the enemy, and nothing will injure you." As the evangelist, He prepared them to go out, protected against the enemies they would face. Furthermore, Jesus told them to bring a blessing of peace wherever they went. They were to sow peace and minister out of peace everywhere they were sent (ref. Luke 10).

Jesus, as the Good Shepherd, revealed the place of security, care, and nurture available to all who enter into His sheepfold through the door of faith in Christ alone. As a shepherd, He reveals and opens the door for listening only to the voice of the Good Shepherd and the ability to discern and turn away from every other voice (ref. John 10). He watches over the sheep and warns of dangers, defends against enemy attacks, and leads into green pastures to receive nutrition that will strengthen and fortify in spirit, soul, and body (ref. Psalm 23). As shepherd, Jesus draws His disciples away with Him to be cared for, nurtured, and protected, especially during seasons of vulnerability, weakness, or weariness. He invites those who follow Him to come up under His shield of faith, reminding me of Psalm 91 and taking refuge under His wings with His truth as both shield and buckler.

Jesus, as teacher, laid foundational truths concerning the reality of the kingdom, its culture, and the *sozo* (salvation, deliverance, and healing) that was afforded to those who are born-again by the Spirit. As teacher, He confronted things they had been taught through the religious system, and He brought His listeners into deeper understanding that produced life. For example, in the Beatitudes, Jesus repeatedly said, "You have heard it said of old, but I say to you...." By so doing, Jesus the teacher released what was needed for the renewing of the mind to think according to God's ways and not the ways of man (ref. Matthew 5). In this role as teacher, Jesus provides a helmet of salvation around the minds of all who will heed His teachings. He takes revelation and unpacks it according to the scriptures so that the fullness of truth is established in the minds of His disciples.

In the fullness of His leadership assignment, Jesus provided protection for those who followed Him in faith and obedience to the things He commanded. As the early disciples submitted to His leadership, they were provided with a firm foundation of truth, righteousness, peace, faith, and salvation and were equipped to walk out the journey of fulfilling their purpose in Christ, standing the tests of faith that came without forsaking the path of life that is found in Christ.

Now having seen the leadership of Jesus as apostle, prophet, evangelist, pastor-shepherd, and teacher as representing strategic ways in which He provides protection for His followers, the pieces of revelation began to make more and more sense. The more I have studied, read and prayed, the more I have seen how God's armor works, and the more I have become convinced that what God was showing me about the armor of God being connected to the grace-gifts of Jesus was valid. Honestly, it is so logical it makes me wonder how I had not seen this before.

In connecting Ephesians 4:11 and Ephesians 6:13-17, the following correlations may be made, as you have seen woven through the previous pages of this book.

Ephesians 4:11	Ephesians 6:13-17
Apostle	Belt of Truth
Prophet	Breastplate of Righteousness
Evangelist	Shoes of Preparation of Gospel of Peace
Pastor-Shepherd	Shield of Faith
Teacher	Helmet of Salvation
The Body of Christ	Sword of the Spirit

For our purposes here, we will not go into depth of teaching of each of these functions, as there are many other resources available that do that with excellence. However, in the coming chapters, we will consider how each of the primary aspects of Christ's grace-gifts given to the church function as the armor. Then, we will look at how, as the corporate body, we wield the sword of the spirit against the forces of darkness over cities, states, regions, and nations. We truly are stronger together than apart!

Please note that I do not believe that this is the only understanding of the armor, but I do believe that this revelation provides a piece of understanding that can certainly help us move forward together as the body of Christ, properly aligned under His five-fold leadership anointings. Our relationship with God always grows out of our personal relationship through Christ our Savior and Lord; therefore, the personal application of the armor is always valid and necessary. However, I am convinced that Holy Spirit desires for us to move into a deeper revelation and subsequent operation as the corporate body of Christ that is to be fully armored with the armor of God.

Questions for Your Consideration

I. What other examples can you think of that depict Jesus' leadership as apostle, prophet, evangelist, teacher, and pastor-shepherd?

II. How do you see the leadership ministry graces of Jesus being manifested in the church today?

III. What questions do you hope to discover answers to regarding the five-fold leadership graces and the corporate armor of God?

A Prayer for You to Pray

Lord,

As we continue on this journey, I ask that You would open the eyes of my understanding to know You more fully so that I might more fully align with You, Your kingdom, and Your purposes through the church to advance the kingdom on earth as it is in heaven. Reveal to me any areas where I need to mature, where my belief systems need to be adjusted, and where my faith needs to be strengthened. I want to be fully aligned, prepared, positioned, and empowered by faith to be all You have purposed for me as a vital member of Your body.

Amen.

SECTION 2

THE CORPORATE ARMOR OF GOD

5 APOSTLES AND PROPHETS

THE BELT OF TRUTH AND THE BREASTPLATE OF RIGHTEOUSNESS

Stand firm therefore, having girded your loins with truth, and having put on the breastplate of righteousness.
                                    Ephesians 6:14

And He gave some as apostles, and some as prophets....
                                    Ephesians 4:11

THESE FIRST TWO GRACE-GIFTS and pieces of the armor of God are so intricately connected, it seems logical to approach these together. Both are foundational to the building and protection of the body of Christ. Ephesians 2:20 speaks of the church being built upon the foundation of apostles and prophets with Jesus Christ as the chief cornerstone. Then, in 1 Corinthians 12:28, Paul writes: "And God has appointed in the church, first apostles, second prophets...." This reveals God's set order in the church, foundational according to God's plan. Some translations read "in the church" and others "for the church," speaking to the position and function. Apostles and prophets, as well as the other grace-gifts of Christ, are placed in the church for Christ's purposes to serve in providing the function ordained by God.

God has ordained that apostles and prophets work together in tandem with each other to produce a solid foundation, securing protection for the body of Christ that positions the church—the ekklesia—to advance in truth and righteousness. Unfortunately, what we have seen far too often is a separation, even antagonism at times, between these two foundational functions. The friction caused by issues such as immaturity, misunderstanding of gift or function, unhealed rejection issues, struggles with pride, control, or vain imaginations, jealousy, envy, and competitiveness have caused a weakness where God intended there to be strength. As we come into increased revelation, understanding, and wisdom regarding God's plan and purposes, I believe we will begin to see a multiplied function that will produce a strength among all of God's people to be and do what He has ordained, securely armored in the corporate armor.

APOSTLES AS THE BELT OF TRUTH

Apostles first in order, in function, in appointment and place, are positioned to provide protection and a secure foundation that is intimately aligned with Jesus Christ, the Chief Cornerstone and fullness of the armor of God. Apostles, not identified by title but by function, not known for prominent position or fame but by the fruit of the body of Christ maturing as each member is equipped (aligned and prepared) to do the work of ministry. Apostles lay a foundation of truth so that the body of Christ is secured to live life by the truth found in Christ, lining up with the plumbline of the Word of God and living by the Spirit of

Truth. Apostles serve as an expression of the belt of truth securing the foundational elements of the gospel of the kingdom so that future generations receive the purity of the gospel that produces passion and power to fulfill purpose.

As we discussed earlier, the belt of truth fits around the body much like a girdle, surrounding the loins—the seat of the seed of future inheritors—with security. Therefore, we see that truth protects the ongoing life and hope for the future generations to be conceived and brought forth to fullness of life.

The belt of truth speaks of guarding against error, compromise, or deception infiltrating the life of the church, as individual members and also for the corporate body. Without the protection of truth, ungodly belief systems and practices can work their way into the body, causing weakness or even death. Furthermore, we see that even as the belt was foundational to the soldiers' armor in the days of Rome, truth serves as a secure foundation for the remainder of the armor. Clearly, we can see that the early apostles functioned in both establishing truth and in guarding against error, compromise, and deception creeping into the fledgling, yet rapidly expanding early church.

For example, in 2 Peter 1:12-13, the Apostle Peter says to his spiritual sons, "Therefore, I will always be ready to remind you of these things, even though you already know them, and have been established in the truth which is present with you. I consider it right, as long as I am in this earthly dwelling, to stir you up by way of reminder." Peter, functioning as an apostle, was alerted and concerned over the battles that were raging against the church in its early days, and he wrote to admonish and remind them to remember and stand in the truth they had learned.

As an apostle, Peter functioned in establishing and guarding truth as a foundation in the early church. His writings continue to secure us in kingdom truth, even as a belt girded around us to protect, secure, and create a foundational piece of armor for the church—the corporate body of Christ.

The belt of truth speaks to those given as grace-gifts as apostles; they are set in place by Christ as foundational to the building of the church. Apostles and apostolic leaders are wise master builders given to the church for the equipping of the saints.

The Apostle Paul, in 1 Corinthians 3:10-22, speaks of functioning as a "wise master builder" laying a foundation upon which others will build upon it. He goes on to discuss the care that is necessary for building on the foundation and how each person's work will be tested. Then, in verse 18, he writes, "Let no man deceive himself...." He drops the plumbline of truth, which functions as an expression of the belt of truth securing the building of the church as the dwelling place of God.

The word in Ephesian 4:12 that is translated as "equipping" is *katartismos*, and it speaks of aligning or adjusting, much like a chiropractor. It can refer to mending or resetting, as in a broken bone. It also speaks of perfecting, as in preparing and maturing, so that the believers are completely adequate or sufficient for the purposes of God. Apostles function to bring proper alignment, preparation, and at times, correction so that there is strength of function within the body, with each part "being fitted and held together by what every joint supplies, according to the proper working of each individual part, causes the growth of the body for the building up of itself in love" (Ephesians 4:16).

We see an example of correction in 1 Corinthians 5 when the Apostle Paul brought a word of rebuke to the church in Corinth for tolerating immortality "of such a kind as does not exist even among the Gentiles." He goes on to set in motion the resetting of proper order and function (*katartismos*) of the church. He was protecting the body from the consequences of allowing tolerance of sin to go unchecked, and he was mending the broken places, even setting a belt of truth around the loins that would strengthen and provide time for healing and restoration to occur.

Later in 2 Corinthians 2, we see Paul speaking the truth of forgiveness and restoration to the church to protect so that "no advantage would be taken of us by Satan, for we are not ignorant of his schemes." This action was another function of both protection against Satan and further equipping the believers for every good work by establishing reconciliation and restoration into the foundation.

Apostles, functioning as the belt of truth for the corporate body of Christ, work to strengthen, mature, align and prepare the saints of God by establishing truth as a plumbline for the whole. Truth speaks of Jesus, the Word of God, and Holy Spirit who is the Spirit of Truth. One of the other functions of apostles, functioning as the belt of truth, is to work with the body to mature it into accurate understanding, processing, and application of the prophetic words that are received both individually and as the corporate body of Christ. As apostles work together with prophets in aligning the body of Christ with the truth of what God is saying and has purposed, strength and confidence to advance rises around the body.

Just as in the armor of God the belt of truth is intricately connected to the breastplate of righteousness, so it is with the grace-gifts of the apostle and prophet. Ephesians 2:20 says, "So then you are no longer strangers and aliens, but you are fellow citizens with the saints, and are of God's household, having been built on the foundation of the apostles and prophets, Christ Jesus Himself being the cornerstone, in whom the whole building is fitted together, is growing into a holy temple in the Lord." This leads us quite easily to the next piece of the armor: the breastplate of righteousness.

Apostles today will challenge the way we think, just as Jesus did. When Jesus was preaching the gospel of the kingdom, He would often say something like, "you have heard it said of old, but I say to you...." Then He would present kingdom truth that confronted the religious truths of the day. Likewise, those with apostolic grace challenge the religious teachings of our day with kingdom wisdom and revelation—kingdom truth—so that we can be more fully protected against the deceiving messages that bombard us each and every day.

I can remember the first time I heard Apostle Clay Nash make the statement, "Trust is a choice; respect can be lost." What? Did I hear him right? I have always heard that trust had to be earned. His statement brought a challenge to what I had been told was "said of old" and led me into kingdom understanding and other measures of relational maturity.

We need apostolic leaders who challenge status quo mediocrity and long-held religious mindsets that are often based more on our traditions and experiences of church and the ways of the world than in the Word of God and the ways of the kingdom.

God has given apostles to secure kingdom realities to protect and gird us so that as we continue on this journey of faith, personally and corporately, we won't go astray or find ourselves built upon a faulty foundation that could easily crumble under the storms of life. Corporately, this becomes exceedingly crucial as we move out to share the gospel of the kingdom and labor with Christ to see His purposes fulfilled on the earth. Without the belt of truth secured by alignment with authentic apostolic authority, the pressures and assaults of the world and the schemes of Satan can erode the integrity of our message, lives, and mission.

PROPHETS AND THE BREASTPLATE OF RIGHTEOUSNESS

The next piece of the armor, the breastplate of righteousness, provides protection over some of the most vital organs of the body, including the heart and lungs. The breastplate, identified by righteousness, provides a significant key as to what will protect us against the wiles of the devil. Satan and his demonic hordes, which emanate out of the kingdom of darkness, are devoid of any semblance of righteousness and are on a mission to destroy God's people through attacks that lure us into unrighteousness, compromise, and vulnerability in any way possible. The enemy knows that a breach of righteousness weakens and can even destroy the life and witness of God's people.

The breastplate of righteousness guards against infiltration into the heart of man. Scripture tells us in Matthew 12:34 (NKJV), "For out of the abundance of the heart the mouth speaks." Therefore, protecting the heart in righteousness is critical if our words are to be filled with the very life of God flowing out of us. Having our hearts protected, both by righteousness and for righteousness' sake, positions us to effectively speak and demonstrate the power of Christ's saving grace.

True prophets of God release words of truth that point to the way of righteousness, most often speaking directly to the heart of the matter. We have all seen, and perhaps chuckled at, the cartoon depictions of prophets with the long-pointed finger. While we do not advocate the judgmentalism that those cartoons often imply, it is true that prophets carry a mandate to speak words that are life-giving through exhortation, encouragement, and edification (ref. 1 Corinthians 14:3). The words of prophets point the way to righteousness, holiness, purpose, and yes, will bring correction when needed. Prophets speak words that guard and protect the very heart of man, pointing in the direction of God's purposes and original intent for a person, organizations, regions and nations. Their words communicate the heart of our Heavenly Father to keep us moving forward in the ways of God, and they keep us from veering off the paths of righteousness that could lead to avoidable pitfalls, battles, and even defeat.

Corporately, prophets release revelation that provides protection against the intrusion of evil from within and without, warning of coming dangers, and pointing the way into the purposes of God for the times and seasons that are at hand. Likewise, as the breastplate of righteousness protects against infiltration of the enemy's tactics to destroy the life and testimony of an individual, so prophets do for the corporate body of Christ.

Amos 3:7 states, "Certainly the Lord God does nothing unless He reveals His secret plan to His servants the prophets." As God reveals His secret plan—His plans, purposes, and intentions—to prophets; courage, strength, confidence, clarity, strategy, direction, and much more flood the heart of man. The revelation of the plans of God strengthens the heart, secures the way of the Lord, and releases faith for God's people to boldly advance against the schemes of the enemy that constantly seeks to undermine the purposes of God.

As the word of the Lord comes through God's servants the prophets, faith comes, and as we allow His words to work in us, we are moved into greater measures of righteousness—not just right-living, but being rightly aligned and positioned by faith to be who God says we are and to do what He has purposed.

Prophets, in their functional leadership, will at times bring correction or warning to guard the body from falling prey to the ploys of the enemy. Perhaps, more importantly, they provide direction on how the church is to move forward in the purposes of the Lord. Prophets speak to the purpose of the whole and to the individual members on their portion of the whole. The leadership function of the prophet as a breastplate of righteousness guards and protects the motivations, intentions, and agendas of the heart according to the purposes of God in righteousness, truth, and justice.

In the book of Acts, Agabus is identified as a prophet. In Acts 11, he brings a word regarding an impending famine all over the world. This prophetic word provided a warning of what was coming, providing an opportunity for the church to prepare and provide assistance to those living in Judea. The disciples rallied to the word and sent supplies by Barnabas and Saul.

Further along in Acts 21, we see Paul arriving in Caesarea and entering into the home of Philip the evangelist, who also had four daughters who were prophetesses. Taking advantage of Paul's visit to the area, Agabus comes down from Judea to deliver the word of the Lord to Paul. This word is a serious warning of dangers that await the apostle.

"And he [Agabus] came to us and took Paul's belt and bound his own feet and hands, and said, "This is what the Holy Spirit says: 'In this way the Jews in Jerusalem will bind the man who owns this belt and hand him over to the Gentiles.'"

Acts 21:11 NASB

Fear immediately gripped those gathered with Paul, and they tried to convince him that he should not go to Jerusalem. However, Paul allowed the word to prepare him to face what was coming and to be strengthened in his inner man to not run or shrink back from fulfilling the purposes of the Lord.

Remember the first prophet that Paul, then known as Saul, heard from was Ananias whom God had told, "Go, for he is a chosen instrument of Mine, to bear My name before the Gentiles and kings and the sons of Israel; for I will show him how much he must suffer for My name's sake" (Acts 9:15).

Saul had just had a life-changing encounter with the Lord, was sitting there blinded and waiting to see what this man sent from God would say to him, and he was given a word about how much he must suffer through being a chosen vessel of the Lord to touch many. Wow! I wonder how many would embrace such a word? Or, would there be an outcry against the word and the prophet?

From the beginning of Paul's journey, God used prophets as a breastplate of righteousness to speak words that would prepare, propel, and help to protect the very core of his being against the assaults that would seek to take him out of fulfilling the purposes of the Lord. The same is true today. God uses prophets to speak words with the very purpose of providing armor around the heart.

In the later part of 2009, the Lord had a prophet deliver a word to me that revealed the scheme of the enemy to do me grave harm. As the prophetic word continued, this woman of God said, "And God says if you don't get about doing the thing I have called you to, he will be successful." The one delivering this word stepped back, looked at me quite intently and said, "And if the enemy is successful, I am going to be very upset with you!" (A little humor both drove home the point and lightened a very intense moment.)

Immediately, Holy Spirit began to speak to me about what it was I wasn't doing, or actually about how I was attempting to do what He had said but in my own way. Ouch!

In the days ahead, as I surrendered and sought the Lord for the path to walk in full obedience to His will in His way, not mine, He began to reorder my life in ways that only He could do. And I am certain that embracing this timely word, "putting on the breastplate of righteousness" delivered through a prophet, saved my life, whether physically or in death to the abundant life-journey of prophetic purpose, only God knows. Today, I am walking in the path of righteousness that God has purposed for my life and give God thanks for sending a prophet with a sure word to speak into my life.

APOSTLES AND PROPHETS TOGETHER

As the breastplate of righteousness connects to the belt of truth in the armor, so also the prophet connects directly to the apostle. Ephesians 2:20 declares that the church is being "built on the foundation of the apostles and prophets." The relationship between apostles and prophets functionally creates an expression of wisdom and revelation intimately working together to form a sure foundation. When prophets and apostles labor together with the revelation of the Lord, interpretation of the revelation comes forth in a greater measure and gives way for the application and implementation through the development of strategies, blueprints and assignments.

This strategic alignment between apostles and prophets in the corporate armor provides a powerful protection for the body of Christ. As prophets come forth with revelation from the Lord and partner together with apostles, the synergy of the grace-gifts produces clarity of direction and also a powerful protection around the body of Christ to move forward in truth and righteousness, withstanding and powerfully advancing against the "gates of hell" (ref. Matthew 16:18).

In 2 Peter 2, the Apostle Peter boldly addresses the issues surrounding false prophets who introduce destructive heresies, and he issues a strong warning about those who follow their ways. Peter defines their ways by the Greek word *apōleia*, which is defined as "pertaining to perdition, destruction, waste, to perish, or pernicious." When we look at the root word, *apollymi*, we glean some deeper understanding, especially as it relates to the dangers of false prophetic ministry. The word means, "to destroy, to put out of the way entirely, abolish, put an end to ruin; render useless, to kill, to perish, to be lost, ruined, destroyed, to mar." Some phrases in Thayer's Greek Lexicon jumped out at me in particular: "to put out of the way entirely, render useless, cause its emptiness to be perceived."

In other words, prophetic ministry needs to be processed properly and connected to truth. False prophets often give accurate words but with wrong motives attached, which is divination. Such words produce destruction and can lead toward loss to those who embrace such words.

Apostles, working together with prophets, are vital to rightly discerning the validity, motive, and authenticity of prophetic words, thus protecting the body from the intrusion of divination, deception, and even delusion.

On the other hand, prophetic words may be accurate, yet when improperly interpreted and applied through filters other than truth—filters such as rejection, unresolved pain, or deception regarding one's own self—the results can be the destruction and waste of the spiritual impact of the word. It is essential for the protection of the purposes of God within individuals and the body of Christ that the belt of truth be securely in place as a firm foundation.

Once we come into an understanding of apostles as representing the belt of truth for the corporate body, we begin to see how the body is protected against deception, delusion, and schemes of the enemy that are set to divert, derail, diminish, and even destroy the body of Christ. Certainly, we know the enemy cannot and will never be able to fully destroy the body of Christ, but we also see clear evidence of much destruction among the endeavors of the body of Christ in pursuit of doing the bidding of the Lord. The belt of truth activated around the body of Christ through apostles providing the grace-gift leadership Christ has bestowed through them is greatly needed.

We can also see how the integrity of the foundational truths of the kingdom found in the Word of God, and the proceeding revelation of prophetic words, are secured through apostolic leaders functioning as a belt of truth for the body, providing leadership to enable solid interpretation, application and implementation of strategies, prophetic words, and teachings within the context of the whole, and not simply as islands unto ourselves. So that every joint will be properly positioned and functioning to cause growth of the whole in love.

Apostles and prophets authentically functioning together provide vitally important protection of the body to walk in righteousness and truth, pursuing and advancing the purposes of Christ and His kingdom throughout the earth. As these two leadership grace-gifts link together in proper alignment, rooted in humility, honor, and love, I am truly convinced that we will see a strength and vitality of grace and authority rise in the church that we have yet to see.

Questions for Your Consideration

I. How would you describe the function of the apostles as an expression of the belt of truth? Can you think of examples of when apostolic leaders have spoken kingdom truth that brought you into greater understanding with Christ and His kingdom?

II. How would you describe the leadership grace of the prophet functioning as the breastplate of righteousness? Think of any examples of prophetic revelation that have brought you into increased righteousness of life as you have allowed the word of the Lord to have its way in and through you.

III. Have you seen apostles and prophets working together in ways that provide protection to the body of Christ in practical ways?

A Prayer for You to Pray

Father,

Thank You for the wisdom and revelation that is given to us through Your apostles and prophets, I acknowledge our need for greater measures of Your leadership grace-gifts to be activated and embraced by the church. Forgive us, Lord, for the ways we have rejected and not put on the fullness of the protective armor that You have provided, both personally and corporately. Help me, Lord, to recognize, rightly discern, and align myself with the fullness of Your body and Your kingdom leadership, so that I and those You have ordained that I be connected to within Your body, might in a greater measure fulfill Your purposes on the earth. In Jesus' name.

Amen.

6 EVANGELIST

THE SHOES OF PREPARATION OF THE GOSPEL OF PEACE

And having shod your feet with the preparation of the gospel of peace.

Ephesians 6:15

And He gave some as apostles, and some as prophets, and some as evangelists....

Ephesians 4:11

THE EVANGELIST IS THEN ADDED to the apostles and prophets, providing the thrust to go out into the world, a world that is filled with anything but peace. The evangelist is prepared to go, created for movement, and is rarely satisfied to stay put anywhere for very long! This one is fearless and radically captivated by the love of God that constrains them to do nothing less than carry the gospel of peace to those who are bound in the bondages of a world that is filled with death, destruction, and deception.

Without the leadership dynamics of the evangelist, we could easily become stagnant and ingrown, losing the thrust of Jesus' mandate to "go into all the world." *Go…!*

Go make disciples.

Go heal the sick.

Go teach to obey.

Go heal the brokenhearted.

Go make disciples of all nations.

Go into all the world and set captives free.

Go!

EVANGELIST AS THE SHOES OF THE PREPARATION OF THE GOSPEL OF PEACE

Evangelists, within the context of the kingdom leadership dynamics of Ephesians 4, are leaders and equippers. They are ones who prepare the "saints for the work of ministry," just as the other leadership dynamics functions do. They are not just those who evangelize but are those who provide leadership training and equipping to prepare and position the saints to do the work of proclaiming the good news.

In Matthew 10, we see a clear picture of Jesus operating in kingdom leadership authority with those who were following Him. Looking with a perspective of the five-fold leadership dynamics that are recorded in Ephesians 4:11, you can see aspects of all five dynamics in this scenario. This becomes clear in Luke 10.

After this, the Lord Jesus formed thirty-five teams among the other disciples. Each team was two disciples, seventy in all, and he commissioned them to go ahead of him into every town he was about to visit. He released them with these instructions:

"The harvest is huge and ripe. But there are not enough harvesters to bring it all in. As you go, plead with the Owner of the Harvest to drive out into his harvest fields many more workers. Now, off you go! I am sending you out even though you feel as vulnerable as lambs going into a pack of wolves. You won't need to take anything with you—trust in God alone. And don't get distracted from my purpose by anyone you might meet along the way.

"Once you enter a house, speak to the people there and say, 'God's blessing of peace be upon this house!' If a lover of peace resides there, your peace will rest upon that household. But if you are rejected, your blessing of peace will come back upon you. Don't feel the need to shift from one house to another, but stay put in one home during your time in that city. Eat and drink whatever they serve you. Receive their hospitality, for you are my harvester, and you deserve to be cared for.

"When you enter into a new town, and you have been welcomed by its people, follow these rules: Eat what is served you. Then heal the sick, and tell them all, 'God's kingdom realm has arrived and is now within your reach!' But when you enter a city and they do not receive you, say to them publicly, 'We wipe from our feet the very dust of your streets as a testimony before you! Understand *this: God's kingdom realm came within your reach and yet you have rejected God's invitation!'"*

Jesus continued, "Let me say it clearly: on the day of judgment the wicked people of Sodom will have a lesser degree of judgment than the city that rejects you, for Sodom did not have the opportunity that was given to them."

Luke 10:1-12 TPT

Jesus prepared and positioned his disciples to go out into the harvest fields, fully equipped for every good work that was ahead of them. He sent (apostle). He gave revelation (prophet). He pointed to the harvest (evangelist). He shepherded them to trust in God alone (pastor). He gave instruction (teacher). The primary emphasis in this passage, however, was that of the evangelist focusing on the harvest and positioning the laborers to be sent out into the harvest fields.

As we read further down in this passage, we discover another key aspect of the evangelist going out into the harvest fields. Jesus clearly reveals the dangers and vulnerabilities (ref. Luke 10:3-4). Then upon their return, when they were ecstatic with joy over the demonstrations of power they had seen, He assures them of the protection and authority they have been given in Luke 10:19:

"Behold, I have given you authority to tread on serpents and scorpions, and over all the power of the enemy, and nothing will injure you."

The word for *tread*, or *trample* in the KJV, is *pateō*, which means "to trample, crush with the feet, to advance by setting foot upon, tread upon: to encounter successfully the greatest perils from the machinations and persecutions with which Satan would fain (being obliged or constrained; compelled to) thwart the preaching of the gospel" (Strong's #G3961).

The word *serpent* references a snake or one who operates in cunning deceitfulness and wisdom (earthly and demonic) to thwart the purposes of God, with a clear reference to the serpent who deceived Eve. Obviously, this is a reference to Satan who appeared as a serpent to deceive Eve in the garden. It can also reference or give understanding to the spirit of python that speaks of a spirit of divination, as seen in Acts 9. In the Old Testament, we also see the use of *serpent* referencing the dangers of poisonous, venomous creatures set to bring destruction but that God grants victory over through His grace (ref. Psalm 91:13 and Isaiah 11:8).

Scorpion speaks of a creature that, though small, has the ability to sting with piercing pain. The word for scorpion is derived from words that reference "peering, watching, striking a mark, concealing, or piercing." The enemy sets himself to inflict pain, suffering, defeat, and devastation through his piercing strikes that are intended to stop us from pursuing the purposes of God. His tactics are typically sneaky, seemingly small yet painful jabs that take us by surprise. Praise God for the shoes of the gospel of peace that protect us from the unseen dangers along our path.

Finally, Christ declared "authority over all the power of the enemy." The word for enemy in this passage is *echthros*, and means "to hate, either aggressively as in blatant hostility, or passively as in attitudes and subtle actions that are oppositional, abhorrent, appalling, scandalous, or revolting." This provides us insight as to the enemy's means of attack and provides assurance that Christ has given us all that we need to overcome his vile attacks no matter how subtle or how blatant they may be.

The Apostle Paul, in writing to the Romans, assured them of victory when he wrote in Romans 16:20 TPT, "And the God of peace will swiftly pound Satan to a pulp under your feet! And the wonderful favor of our Lord Jesus will surround you." Notice it is the God of peace, which reveals that it is peace that overcomes the enemy; and it is the gospel of peace shod upon our feet that releases God's "swift pounding" of Satan through us as we go out into the world to share the marvelous good news of Christ and His kingdom.

One incredibly fascinating nugget regarding the word *peace* that is used in Romans 16:20 and Ephesians 6:15. The Greek word is *eirene* which according to Strong's concordance means: "1. a state of national tranquility, exemption from the rage and favor of war; 2. Peace between individuals, I.e., harmony, concord; 3. Security, safety, prosperity, felicity," (because peace and harmony make and keep things safe and prosperous). It further references the peace of Messiah and the way that leads to peace; of Christianity and the peace of soul that comes through our union with Christ; and ultimately the state of peace after death.

In this, we see the ultimate and progressive implications of the gospel of peace on individuals and regions or nations. As our feet are shod with the preparation of the gospel of peace, we go forth protected and empowered to overcome, trample, and crush the enemy under our feet, and to set captives free to enter into the blessings that come through faith in Jesus Christ our Lord.

As evangelists partner together with the apostles and prophets, the body of Christ will be more thoroughly equipped, prepared, and released to strategically advance the kingdom effectively against the schemes and plots of the enemy. Evangelists properly positioned within Christ's leadership expression keep the whole body moving forward with a harvest mentality. Christ also provides protection from places and situations that are outside the timing and specific assignments of the Lord.

We must remember that if the enemy cannot keep us from following the Lord, he will often attempt to entice us to go out beyond the scope, authority, and metron of the measure Christ has given us at any particular point in time. Evangelists properly positioned with apostles and prophets secure the walk and advancement by the apostolic foundation of truth and the prophetic revelation of righteousness. And, as was stated previously, having the evangelist fully active within the kingdom leadership structure will keep us all moving forward with a harvest mentality.

It is important to note that the language of this particular piece of the armor is quite interesting and revealing. With the belt of truth, breastplate of righteousness, shield of faith, and helmet of salvation, we are told to put it on, as we are the "shoes of the preparation of the gospel of peace." The difference is that it is the shoes of the preparation, not just the shoes of the gospel of peace. We know God doesn't say anything or use words for no reason, so there must be a reason for this distinction.

The word *preparation*, in the original Greek language, is *hetoimasia*, and means "the act of preparing, the condition of a person or thing so far both as prepared, preparedness, readiness." It comes from the word, *hetoimazō*, meaning "to make ready, prepare, to make the necessary preparation, get everything ready." When you take this word to its root, it has to do with "fitness."

The word for *shod* is *hypodeō* and means "to underbind, to bind under one's self, or bind on." It comes from two words that mean "to bind, tie, or fasten" and "under." So we are to adhere to the gospel of peace to have its full work in us, securely fastened underneath our feet, our walk, submitting to the process of preparation, and making everything ready and fit for the work of ministry that lies ahead.

Only as the gospel of peace works in us, bringing forth liberty from the havoc, rigors, and confusion of all that seeks to disrupt and destroy God's purposes and plans in us, will we be thoroughly equipped for the good work of evangelism, taking the message of Good News to those who are desperately in need of the "peace of God that surpasses all understanding" through Christ Jesus (ref. Philippians 4:6).

FUNCTION AND TESTIMONY

Admittedly, the leadership grace-gift of evangelist is my personal weakest grace, yet it is a passion of my heart to see those who are lost, who have gone astray, or who are in the throes of deep bondage, to be redeemed and walking in the fullness of all God has intended for their lives. Those graced as evangelists inspire and challenge me. And I am grateful!

Evangelists supernaturally see the harvest and are graced with a boldness born of passionate love, to go into places and situations with the love of Jesus. A young couple in our ministry, Nathanael and Tiffany, carry the heart of the evangelist and have been known to go where many of us would have feared to venture. For years God met them in these places of evangelism, manifesting great signs, wonders, and miracles as they took the gospel of peace into extremely dark and demonically infested places. However, they would often suffer great setbacks after their adventures and found that the zeal of their heart yearned for alignment with kingdom leaders who could help bring them into greater measures of Christ's call for their lives.

Today, after several years of walking in alignment within our apostolic center, allowing the kingdom leadership gifts to help them to mature and develop more fully, they are now emerging as kingdom leadership graced as evangelist, and will undoubtedly help many, not just come into the kingdom, but to find their place of alignment, activation, and advancement. Below is a portion of their testimony that I believe will encourage many.

My wife, Tiffany, and I both survived the wild and reckless pursuit of pleasure throughout our childhood and teenage years. If we were to be honest, our quest with other prodigals was really about finding peace rather than some obscure, temporary pleasure. Within the dark nightclubs, raves, and warehouses, we joined thousands of other lost souls trying to find relief from the terrors of a life without Jesus. There was loud music, flashing lights, alcohol, drugs, and countless souls trying to silence the groan and ache coming from the God-sized hole in their lives. We drank deeply from that horrible cup for years, but God's mercy ripped us out of the grip of death numerous times and delivered us from the cycles of sin and brokenness.

When Tiffany and I met at the end of 2007, we quickly found out that we shared a mutual love for dance music with a growing desire to reach the children of the night through God's love. We dreamed and planned as friends, and then in 2009 became married partners in this venture. We started throwing small worship events with dance music to gather our tribe, and soon after we found ourselves leading teams into some of the largest dance music festivals in the world.

We saw good fruit the first two years; then we aligned with Apostle Jacquie and the CityGate Atlanta family. The spiritual shift we experienced was far from a placebo effect. Everything changed. Strategies became more dynamic, divine appointments were more frequent, healings and miracles increased, and our authority level was now shutting darkness down, not just dispelling it.

One of the largest electronic music festivals in the world (over 50,000 from many nations in attendance) had been coming to Atlanta for two years, bringing witchcraft, sorcery, and all manner of wickedness. Within the first two years that we went, we saw enough fruit to justify our return the following year. However, the year we aligned with Apostle Jacquie we had providence lead us to a behind-the-scenes tour before the event started. We walked the land and prayed, as CityGate Atlanta and Apostle Jacquie covered us in decrees and intercession. That night, a downpour came, flooding one of the massive parking lots. Confusion filled the enemy's camp as we ministered the next two days, and the weekend ended with this festival shut down, bankrupt, and never to return to our city again.

We also began taking teams into some of the most satanic nightclubs and raves in the city of Atlanta. On one particular Halloween night, we were asked by a secular promoter to set up a "Dream Interpretation and Spiritual Readings Booth" within their event. It was helpful to have an apostolic counsel to determine if this was God's doing or a trap. We learned to not be the presumptuous type of evangelists. With CityGate Atlanta's partnership, we were ministering healing and prophetic words in one space, while a seance was going on in a neighboring room within the rave. Our presence disrupted psychic booths and all of the inferior counterfeits that darkness was manifesting. We had an open heaven while Apostle Jacquie and the intercessors of CGA stayed awake to pray for us until about three in the morning. Soon after, that demonic rave club was shut down and didn't reopen.

Apostolic alignment was also about being equipped. Apostle Jacquie set leaders around us with tools that we needed, such as Winston and Pat Harvey who lead Restoring the Foundations in this region. The tools we gained from the leaders at CityGate, such as RTF, brought our personal ministry experiences to another level. When we traveled to events outside of America, like a festival in Mexico, we saw so many healings occur, that a line formed. Our team ministered for hours every day, because we took what we learned and applied it in whatever setting the Lord placed us. Alignment was about connection that brought an exchange of life. This exchange caused an increased manifestation of the nature of God in our midst. As the Apostle Paul said, it was "faith working through love," and the final result was His kingdom come and His divine will fulfilled through a family synergized and interconnected by an apostolic fastening of the body in all its moving parts. This is what my wife, Tiffany, likes to affectionately call "The Transforming Power of Alignment."

CONCLUSION

Clearly, the body of Christ needs our feet shod with the preparation of the gospel of peace to be protected and empowered to go forth into the world, trampling on the enemy so that captives will be set free and the harvest is secured out of the grips of the enemy's ensnaring traps.

As the evangelists, as kingdom leaders, take their place among Christ's leadership, the corporate body will be properly shod to move out into new territories, protected from the slithering, lurking, deceptive traps of the enemy. We will also be securely fitted upon the firm foundation of the peace of God and the God of peace that crushes Satan under our feet. We will no longer be bound inside the four walls of the church, but prepared and secured to advance the kingdom of God in power.

QUESTIONS FOR YOUR CONSIDERATION

I. How would you describe the "Shoes of the preparation of the gospel of peace" in your own words? Is there anything you are seeing differently about this piece of armor than you have in the past? If so, what difference do you believe this will make in your life?

II. Take a moment to consider the "preparation" aspect of the shoes and the function of the evangelists as one of the vital aspects of Christ's delegated kingdom leadership. How do you believe this understanding can affect the way the church operates?

III. How do you believe having the evangelist firmly secured as a part of the armor will help mature the church to more effectively advance the kingdom in our day?

A PRAYER FOR YOU TO PRAY

Almighty God,

Open the eyes of my understanding and activate my heart to see the harvest that is all around me. I am asking for the activation and increased function of Christ's leaders, the evangelists, within the kingdom leadership structures of our day. Use the evangelists to help prepare and position us to go forth into the highways and byways of our communities and nations to bring the message of the Good News of peace; not peace as the world gives, but peace that delivers from the havoc and ravages of war, and the turmoil of the kingdom of darkness that constantly seeks to kill, steal, and destroy. Thank You,

Lord, that You have given us all we need to trample over every tactic, scheme and device of the enemy. Victory is ours in Jesus' name.

Amen.

7 PASTOR-SHEPHERD

THE SHIELD OF FAITH

In addition to all, taking up the shield of faith with which you will be able to extinguish all the flaming arrows of the evil one.

Ephesians 6:16

And he has appointed some with grace to be apostles, and some with grace to be prophets, and some with grace to be evangelists, and some with grace to be pastors.

Ephesians 4:11 TPT

IN THE PREVIOUS CHAPTERS we have seen how the apostle, prophet, and evangelist provide armor figuratively covers the vital organs of the body's torso, and the feet as the expression of walking and going out into the world. Now we turn our attention to the pastor, or perhaps better referenced as the role of the shepherd of the household of faith. Pastors are those assigned and graced by Christ to express the watchful care of the Good Shepherd. They carry His heart and compassion to watch over and tend to the sheep of His pasture.

Pastors have historically, within Evangelical Christianity, been the primary role we have seen as leaders in the church. In fact, the term or title "pastor" became synonymous with one who leads the church, took care of the needs of the members, taught the word, visited the sick, counseled the hurting, performed marriages, funerals, managed the church's finances, buildings, staff, volunteers, and a plethora of various and other jobs too numerous to list. It is no wonder that historically pastors resign and go in search of another job or career at a significantly high rate. Recent research does report that this trend is improving, and I would suggest that it is due to an increased understanding of God's order of the Ephesians 4 leadership model being embraced more fully now than at any time since the early centuries of the church.

However, as we look at Ephesians 4:11, we see that the function of pastor or shepherd is listed fourth in sequence, not of importance but pointing to function. Pastors are graced by Christ to "nurture, care for, tend to, strengthen, and protect" the young, the vulnerable, and the wounded, as well as to help care for the soul of all the saints. They are the ones graced to lift up faith over the flock of God, to extinguish the fiery darts of the enemy, and are a tremendous asset to the protection of the body from the schemes of the enemy that would seek to slip in to devour, divide, and destroy.

It's the shepherd who goes after the one when they go astray; who pours oil on the head to protect and soothe with the tender mercies and compassion of Christ. It's the shepherd who binds up the brokenhearted, comforts the weary, and consoles those who are downtrodden and battle weary. Shepherds are much like mother hens who gathers their chicks under their wings to protect them from an impending or raging storm.

Shepherds, rather than being purposed to lead as our cultural understanding has presented, are those called to feed and nurture those within the church to bring the teachings, revelation, and impartations of the apostles and prophets into practicality and maturity among the saints. They also are the ones who take the young believers under their care to faithfully disciple, instruct, encourage, protect, and guide them toward maturity in the ways of the Lord. They care for those wounded in the journey of life or the ravages of spiritual warfare, making sure they are nurtured back to fullness of health and vitality. They also work alongside the apostles, prophets, evangelists, and teachers to help create and nurture healthy relational dynamics of family among the people.

When the sheep are lacking in faith, either due to the immaturity of a young faith or the weariness that can come to any after extended times of testings and trials, they lift up their shield of faith to protect, guard, and shelter. The pastor-shepherd, as one with the Lord who is the source and full expression of faith, becomes an extension of Christ, the shield of faith, over the body.

In Ezekiel 34, God speaks words of correction and promised restoration into the scenario of shepherds who were not caring and leading the sheep the way He intended. God is restoring the shepherd in this hour.

Old Wineskin Pastor-Shepherds	New Wineskin Pastor-Shepherds
Senior leader of the church	A part of the five-fold leadership
Responsible for weekly preaching	Developing and helping to oversee discipleship into kingdom living
People focused	God focused
Needs motivated	Motivated to see all walk with a healthy soul-life
Easily swayed to do whatever is needed to keep the sheep from leaving	Motivated to see all God's people grow and mature into being effective and fruitful
Raising sheep who stay in the sheep pen	Releasing lions who know how to take the gospel of the kingdom into the world
Co-dependence trap based on need-to-be-needed value	Nurturing toward dependence upon the lord and interdependence within the body
Failure to see the kingdom ministry assignments the lord could have for those in their care	Looking to see and help mature the purpose and destiny God has for each person to fulfill all their God-ordained ministry assignments
Can be more focused on representing the sheep to God rather than God to the sheep	Pursues representing the heart of the father to the people that always nurtures according to God's purpose and glory
Can fall into coddling the wounded and oppressed out of compassion	Minister healing and deliverance, and teach how to gain and keep their healing and freedom

One of the challenges I have observed as we are pursuing the restoration of the five-fold leadership graces of Christ to the church, is the need of having the mindsets and expectations associated with pastoring transformed to be more fully aligned with the ways of the kingdom. Unfortunately, under previous expressions of pastoring within the church culture, many pastors succumbed to the cultural pressures and even misguided understanding of what it meant to shepherd God's people. Here are some of the cautions for us as we move forward in five-fold leadership for the pastor-shepherds among us. I am using "Old Wineskin" to speak of the traditional, cultural expressions of church that the majority of us have grown up in, and "New Wineskin" to speak of the restoration of the apostolic model of church that we see rooted in scripture, demonstrated in the early church, and forming again in our day.

Obviously, I do not mean these comparisons to reflect negatively upon pastors in general, but to simply acknowledge some of the traps that we have fallen into over the years that have contributed to a breakdown of kingdom culture, not just in the world but within the church. Without pastors functioning in alignment with the apostles and prophets who operate strongly in truth and righteousness, wisdom and revelation, and with strategies to build according to the revelation of the Lord for His house to advance His kingdom, we end up with compromised doctrines to accommodate personal preferences and ungodly belief systems developed out of wounding, cultural abnormalities, and the perversions of delusion the enemy is consistently seeking to sow among God's people.

We need shepherds who walk in a high level of integrity of faith to preserve, protect, and promote the fullness of the gospel of the kingdom through discipleship and care for the sheep that will help mature them into a full expression of who God created them to be. There are many true shepherds who do just that, and for these, we give thanks and applaud their selfless service to the body of Christ.

Conversely, as the restoration of apostolic and prophetic leaders has been emerging over the last few decades, there have been occurrences where the pastor-shepherd leadership gift has been missing or unfortunately, diminished as having any importance. This resulted, at times, with people moving into some measure of understanding apostolic and prophetic dynamics, but without authentic incorporation into daily life as maturing citizens of the kingdom. At other times, those given by Christ as pastor-shepherds have felt displaced and devalued, or have simply put new titles on the same old ways of doing things.

The lack of true pastor-shepherd leaders functioning as a part of the kingdom leadership, either as a result of the rejection of the pastor-shepherd function or the retitling of the pastor-shepherd to being an apostle, has often left a gaping breach in the corporate armor that God has intended. The shield of faith, as expressed through the kingdom leadership dynamic of the pastor-shepherd, is vital to the body of Christ as we face challenges, attacks, and onslaughts from the enemy. We desperately need those who carry the heart of the Good Shepherd to cover and shield with faith that is active, true, alive, and transformational.

As we have sought to build an apostolic hub here at CityGate Atlanta, we have seen time and time again where the pastors-shepherds have been able to help our overall leadership moving forward with apostolic and prophetic vision while not leaving behind the people God has given to us to lead. Pastor-shepherds ask the questions that lead us to practically and intentionally work to be sure the people are grasping and incorporating the kingdom messages that are being brought forth weekly. Oftentimes, the pastors will hear the voice of the people expressing their questions, concerns, challenges, and concerns before the apostles and prophets. Or, they will observe behaviors and attitudes that indicate the need for more intentional discipleship in an area.

Pastors, when functioning as a part of the kingdom leadership, become a place of safety and security in the midst of challenging times. One of the first times that I shared this revelation, a woman came to me after the service to share a difficult situation that she knew she would be facing within the next week. I called a pastoral couple over to listen to her heart, to pray for her and to assure her that we would be praying for her during the week. The following Sunday, she came in and gave testimony as to how she was able to walk through the situation in faith with greater peace than she had ever believed was possible. The shield of faith was activated and effective!

Questions for Your Consideration

I. How does your experience with pastors agree or differ with what has been presented as the new wineskin model of pastor-shepherd as a part of the full kingdom leadership dynamic Christ gave to the church?

II. When considering the shield of faith, can you think of examples where the pastor-shepherd has strengthened your walk by lifting up the shield of faith over you? Perhaps it was in times of crisis, or just when you needed to grow or mature? Thank God for His pastor-shepherds that watch after the sheep of the household of faith!

III. Think of ways that the pastor-shepherd, operating to provide a shield of faith, could benefit you and the body you are a part of. Begin to pray for these things to be brought forth across the broader body of Christ.

A Prayer for You to Pray

Father,

You sent Jesus as the Good Shepherd and He demonstrated Your heart of care and compassion, strength and fortitude to see those who came to Him in faith to come into the fullness of who You intended them to be; individually and as members of the Household of Faith. Today, I declare honor for those You have given to the church as pastor-shepherds to provide an expression of Your own armor over the body as the shield of faith. Activate the pastors as the shield of faith in our day that we might more effectively quench all the fiery darts of the evil one and be strengthened to advance in full assurance of faith for Your glory and honor. In Jesus' name.

Amen.

8 Teacher

The Helmet of Salvation

And take the helmet of salvation.

Ephesians 6:17

And He gave some as apostles, some as prophets, some as evangelists, some as pastors and teachers.

Ephesians 4:11

WE COME NOW TO THE FIFTH PIECE of the armor of God, the helmet of salvation. The helmet, by its very nature, protects the head or metaphorically, the thinking of man. This final protective piece of the armor provides a vitally important aspect of armor for the body of Christ, completing the protection from head to toe.

Teachers, by their God-given nature, carry a deep passion for the integrity and purity of the Word of God, and for the Word to be properly interpreted, applied, and incorporated into the daily expressions of faith. Christ has graced these with a unique ability and desire to search out the deep and hidden riches of the Word of God. You will often find teachers surrounded by books, books, and more books! Along with concordances, lexicons, Bible dictionaries, biblical encyclopedias, and all manner of study materials.

Teachers have an insatiable hunger to study and make known the riches of God's Word and spiritual understanding. These men and women of God thrive on both study and developing lessons, plans, and ways to communicate truth in biblical, historical, and practical contexts. They love to unpack kingdom concepts in ways that will help others understand the word and ways of God in deeper ways.

Teachers are fascinating in their pursuit of information. God has given them what seems to be an innate radar to ferret out hidden treasures of truth, understanding and wisdom to prove, or disprove, belief systems, revelation, suppositions, or assumptions! These treasure hunters provide vital protection to the body of Christ to help guard and secure the integrity of biblical truth and application.

Teachers provide invaluable service to the ongoing process of maturing into the mind of Christ, for us as individual believers but also for the corporate body of Christ. These kingdom leaders help guard the belief systems of the church against the consistent bombardment of cultural pressures to compromise, reinterpret, and change the solid foundations God has provided through His Word, both written in the Word and released prophetically through the revelatory manifestations of Holy Spirit.

We know that one of the primary ways the enemy attacks, torments, and deceives is through the mind. He whispers thoughts and ideas that are contrary to truth, questions the validity of what God has said, and seeks to sow seeds of deception through various means of misinterpretation, false revelation, and heretical ideologies. It is imperative that our minds be protected by teaching that comes through the grace-gift of Christ the teacher.

When Jesus walked the earth, He confronted traditions of man, erroneous religious teachings, and legalistic practices time and time again. He would say things like "you have heard it said of old, but I say unto you...." Then He would proceed to bring forth kingdom understanding (ref. Matthew 5). By doing so, Jesus confronted misguided, misapplied, erroneous teachings and the traditions of the religious leaders of the day. It angered the religious traditionalists while liberating those seeking to truly know the ways of the Lord.

Today we desperately need kingdom leadership teachers who have the mind of Christ with solid biblically based and revelatory understanding to bring the body into fuller manifestations of the mind of Christ, which is our strongest defense against the mind-attacks of the enemy. When the church is lacking in biblical understanding, there are gaps through which the enemy can infiltrate even the core foundational beliefs that are critical to the faith. Once thoughts, ideologies, and false doctrines are infiltrated into the thinking of the church, it doesn't take long for strongholds of anti-Christ agendas to begin being constructed and accepted by increasing numbers within the church. Eventually, if not stopped, these strongholds become entrenched as normal and accepted beliefs, and truth is trampled.

For instance, there are some long-standing religious beliefs that are accepted by many as solid truth that have become strongholds of the mind that war against biblical truth. Consider beliefs surrounding the manifestation gifts of the Spirit—things like tongues, interpretation of tongues, words of knowledge or wisdom, miracles. Consider other doctrines like women in ministry, allowable music, and baptisms—some sprinkle, some immerse, some baptize infants, some only baptize as an expression of personal faith, some believe in the baptism of Holy Spirit, and some consider it heresy!

Or what about the infiltration of thought based on relativism, humanism, and cultural pressures of the day regarding certain lifestyle choices that are now redefining marriage, undermining the truth of one's biological gender with dysphoria, eroding the role of authority and responsibility in a child's life. The list goes on and on, even within the walls of the church.

The opinions of man, religious traditions, and doctrines of demons consistently pelt the mind of those within the body of Christ and the corporate body, seeking to erode and ultimately destroy.

We desperately need the helmet of salvation securely placed upon our heads!

We need solid kingdom teachers functioning as a part of Ephesians 4:11 leadership to bring forth biblical understanding from a kingdom perspective, saying in a manner like Jesus our teacher, "You have heard it said, but I say unto you...."

The kingdom leadership grace of the teacher provides essential protection to ensure that what we believe is thoroughly rooted and grounded in the Word of God with Holy Spirit revelation and proper exegesis of the Word. As kingdom teachers function within their place among the five-leadership grace-gifts of Christ to the church, the body of Christ will mature with strength and fortitude to stand and withstand the barrage of cultural and demonic mind-attacks that constantly seek to let down our guard and compromise regarding what God has said. Isn't this the tactic Satan has used from the beginning? In Genesis 3:1, the serpent said to the woman: "Has God really said...?" Satan uses the same tactic today, and we must have our minds protected by the helmet of salvation with teachers providing spiritual wisdom and revelation as revealed through the Word and Spirit of God.

Let's briefly look at the helmet of salvation from a corporate perspective. The helmet, as we have previously stated, covers the head or the mind of the body. Without taking this analogy too far, it is interesting to consider that this piece of armor covering or protecting the head can speak of leadership when looking at the body. Obviously, we know that Christ is the only true and ultimate head; but He has given to the church those whom He has graced to serve as leaders representing His leadership. With that in mind, if the head or leadership of the body is unprotected and vulnerable to the assault of the enemy, then the entire body will suffer the effects with the eroding of truth that is to govern the church.

Then, we come to the word for salvation, *sōtērios*, which means: "saving, bringing salvation," or it can reference "defense or defender." Its companion word, *sōtēria*, speaks of "deliverance, preservation, safety, salvation, health, and deliverance from the molestation of enemies" (Strong's G4991, definition 1.A). These come from the root word, *sōtēr*, simply defined as "savior, deliverer, preserver."

Putting these words together, we see the helmet of salvation is that piece of armor that covers and protects the leaders and the mind of the body of Christ, with a specific assignment to protect the mind of those God has chosen to be head (not in preeminence but in the place of responsibility and authority before the Lord) of His body on the earth. This helmet is to bring forth the security, safety, deliverance, and preservation of the body against the onslaught and molestations of enemies that seek to kill, steal, and destroy the very life and authenticity of who the church is designed to be and all she is destined to do to fulfill God's original intent to bring forth the kingdom of God on earth as it is in heaven.

Time and time again, I have seen where wisdom and revelation have been secured in my own thinking, and in that of the church, as anointed teachers have unpacked revelation from the vantage point of one who has searched out the deep things to make it plain to others so that we might all walk together in greater understanding and faith. Robert Heidler, of Glory of Zion, is one of the strongest kingdom leadership teachers of our day. He is especially graced to take the prophetic revelations through Chuck Pierce, a proven prophet of

God, and bring them forth with solid biblical foundations and practical application so that the body might apply the revelation in ways that are true.

Dutch Sheets, an apostle with a strong mantle of a teacher, skillfully breaks down biblical words out of the original language in such a way that both revelation and understanding explode within the hearer. The veins of biblical truth that are revealed and solidified through his strong apostolic teaching gift work to lead the body of Christ into deeper measures of kingdom truth that causes great faith to rise to be the church Christ intends us to be. These teachings also serve to protect the body from going astray or from simply losing heart in seasons of intense warfare.

God is using these two kingdom teachers in powerful ways to help the body keep moving forward in confident assurance that what God has said, He will do based upon the living Word of God. In our day, God is raising up men and women who are given by Christ to His church to release kingdom teaching that will serve as a helmet of salvation for the body in the midst of grave warfare aimed at eroding the very Mind of Christ.

A final comment of caution regarding teachers that comes straight from the Word of God that I believe is vitally important that we remember. James 3:1-2 in The Passion Translation reads this way:

My dear brothers and sisters, don't be so eager to become a teacher in the church since you know that we who teach are held to a higher standard of judgment. We all fail in many areas, but especially with our words. Yet if we're able to bridle the words we say we are powerful enough to control ourselves in every way, and that means our character is mature and fully developed.

As we consider kingdom leadership teachers in light of the corporate armor representing the helmet of salvation, it is wise to take this passion to heart. If we, as teachers, are not able to bridle our own tongues to speak with a purity of heart, motive, and firmly established on the whole counsel of God, we would best be quiet until we come to a depth of maturity that will not cause harm to God's people or do damage to the proclamation of the gospel of salvation. As teachers positioned to protect the integrity of the Word of God, confirming, affirming, and establishing the fullness of God's salvation must be of utmost importance so that the thinking and belief systems of the church are properly established in God's people.

QUESTIONS FOR YOUR CONSIDERATION

I. In your journey of faith, recall times when kingdom teachers asked questions or challenged your belief systems as Jesus did in His day. "You have heard it said, but I say unto you...."

II. Consider current situations facing the church in our day that point out the desperate need for teaching based on the Word and Spirit of God. List some places where the plumbline of the Word of God needs to be restored in the church today in order for the church to move into greater measures of the Mind of Christ.

III. Thank God for the kingdom teachers who are positioned as vital members of the leadership that Christ has given to the church. Pray for the teachers you know to stand strong in truth born of the Word and Spirit in the midst of the onslaughts of the enemy's attacks against God's purposes.

A PRAYER FOR YOU TO PRAY

Almighty God,

Thank You for those whose Christ has graced to be teachers within the body of Christ; empower them by Your Spirit to teach truth with all clarity, conviction, and the authority that is born of the Word and Holy Spirit. Awaken Your church to fully embrace and put on the helmet of salvation by honoring and heeding the vitally important teachings through Your appointed kingdom teachers. Restore in fullness Christ grace-gift of teacher to the kingdom leadership of Your church so that we might all be fully armored and prepared for every good work, and to stand firm against all the schemes of the evil one. In the mighty name of Jesus.

Amen.

9 THE SWORD OF THE SPIRIT

And take...the sword of the Spirit, which is the word of God. With every prayer and request, pray at all times in the Spirit, and with this in view, be alert with all perseverance and every request for all the saints

Ephesians 6:17-18

And take the mighty razor-sharp Spirit-sword of the spoken word of God.

Pray passionately in the Spirit, as you constantly intercede with every form of prayer at all times. Pray the blessings of God upon all his believers.

Ephesians 6:17b-18 TPT

For the word of God is living and active, and sharper than any two-edged sword, even penetrating as far as the division of soul and spirit, of both joints and marrow, and able to judge the thoughts and intentions of the heart.

Hebrews 4:12

The godly ones shall be jubilant in glory;
They shall sing for joy on their beds.
The high praises of God shall be in their mouths,
And a two-edged sword in their hands,

> *To execute vengeance on the nations,*
> *And punishment on the peoples,*
> *To bind their kings with chains,*
> *And their dignitaries with shackles of iron,*
> *To execute against them the judgment written.*
> *This is an honor for all His godly ones.*
> *Praise the Lord!*
>
> Psalm 149:5-9

NOW THAT ALL THE ARMOR is properly fitted upon the body, Paul exhorts us that it is time to take action, to take up the sword of the Spirit and to pray! This is where we, together as the corporate body, the ekklesia, move forward with the Word and prayer as kings and priests unto our God.

Revelation 1:6 says that through Christ, God "has made us kings and priests to His God and Father, to Him be glory and dominion forever and ever. Amen." Again, in Revelation 5:10, it is recorded: "And have made us kings and priests to our God; and we shall reign on the earth." Understanding the dynamic truths that we are "kings and priests" relates directly to taking up the "sword of the Spirit and prayer."

Let's take a look at each for a moment.

KINGS UNTO OUR GOD

Kings rule. Kings reign. Kings govern. Kings issue decrees. Kings go to war against the enemy that would dare seek to cause harm to the domain over which they are to rule. They are commissioned and expected to protect their territories and those who live within the boundaries of their kingdom. They are to watch over and steward what has been entrusted to them. If they do not, they put the realms of their assigned authority at risk and in grave danger.

As kings unto our God, under the ultimate domain of the King of kings and Lord of lords, we are expected to rule, reign, govern, issue decrees, and when necessary to protect their domain, advancing victoriously into new territories to set free all that is held captive by the kingdom of darkness. Jesus, the King above all kings, has granted us authority to do what we have been commissioned to do—to rule and reign on the earth; to go and disciple nations; to set captives free; to advance the kingdom of God throughout the earth.

As kings unto our God, we each have spheres of authority that Christ has given us to rule and reign over, to bring ever-increasing measures of Christ's kingdom "on earth as it is in heaven." We are to bring His kingdom rule of love, power, and a sound mind, in righteousness, peace, and joy into our homes, our families, jobs, neighborhoods, everywhere Christ has established us by His grace.

As kings, we are to represent the will of the King of kings to those in our sphere, naturally and spiritually. We are under His Kingship and commissioned to represent His kingdom rule on the earth. As such, He grants to us a measure of authority in accordance with His will, ways, and purposes to release His dominion into the earth.

PRIESTS UNTO OUR GOD

Overall, being priests unto our God is more recognized and embraced than the role of being kings. Sometimes, in our pursuit of embracing our role as kings, some have minimized or forsaken the vital place of being priests. If I may be so bold, we can never truly be kings without living first as priests.

Our role as priests positions us as those ministering first and foremost to the Lord; caring for what is upon the heart of the Lord; presenting our needs and the needs of others before the Lord in expression of our faith, hope, and dependence upon Him as the source of all that we could need or ask. Priests represent the heart of surrender in worship and intercession. Priests present incense before the altar of the Lord. They tend to the altar to be sure it is not only functional but continually burning with the fire of the Lord in all purity and passion, with the praise and prayers of the saints ascending continually before the Lord.

In Ezekiel 44, we read a pointed description contrasting the priests who went astray when others went astray and the priests (the sons of Zadok) who remained true to the Lord. Those who went astray were prohibited from drawing near to the Lord and were relegated to doing the mundane work of tending to the work of the temple. But those who remained faithful were welcomed in, to minister to the Lord, drawing near to Him. They were able to go and minister to the people, judging in righteousness, ruling in matters of dispute, bringing forth the rule of God and His kingdom into the earth.

KINGS AND PRIESTS

Faithful priests minister to the Lord, presenting the heart and needs of people before the throne of God. We have all been made priests by the blood of Jesus and no longer need to approach God through another man. We have been granted access to come confidently before the throne of grace because of Jesus, the High Priest, who openly welcomes us to draw near (Hebrews 4:14-16).

As we saw in Ezekiel 44, it is the faithful priests who were granted the grace to rule in the affairs of man with the counsel of God. Those were granted authority as an expression of kingship rule.

This union of the kingly and priestly may be seen even more clearly in King David who had a heart after God's own heart. He was a passionate worshipper who demonstrated the order of ministering first unto the Lord and then, ruling as king. It was this heart of worship that God formed in order to establish the Tabernacle of David. In the Tabernacle of David, there were priests positioned night and day to worship and intercede. There were scribes in place to record the praise, worship, prayers, declarations, and decrees received out of prophetic revelation. The Psalms record for us the brilliance and majesty of the priestly and kingly authority being expressed through God's people.

In the Psalms and elsewhere throughout scripture, we see three strands woven together that God has ordained to be released through those He has called as kings and priests. These are praise, prayers, and proclamations.

Praise firmly settles that God alone holds the highest place in our lives and over all things.

Prayers express the cries of our hearts for God's will and purposes to be made known so that He is glorified in and through the people on the earth.

Proclamations, or decrees, express and establish the rule of heaven on earth through the mouth of God's people speaking out what God has ordained.

Psalm 115:16, in the NASB, reads: "The heavens are the heavens of the Lord, but the earth He has given to the sons of mankind." The Passion Translation brings even greater clarity: "The heavens belong to our God; they are His alone, but he has given us the earth and put us in charge. God has given the earth to us—His children—to steward, to rule and reign according to His good pleasure." One of the ways we do this is through proclamations and decrees received through our times of praise and prayer.

Taking Up the Sword and Prayer

As kings and priests unto our God, properly fit and knit together as members of the body of Christ, the corporate one new man, fully armored with the armor of God, we take up the Sword and we pray. We move as kings and priests.

The sword of the Spirit is the Word of God, both the written and the ever-proceeding word of the Lord that God sends forth to reveal what are His will, purpose, and original intentions. We take up those words from God and they become a "sharp two-edged sword in our mouths," according to Psalm 149:5-9, "to execute vengeance on the nations, and punishment on the peoples, to bind their kings with chains, and their dignitaries with shackles of iron, to execute against them the judgment written. This is an honor for all His godly ones."

Throughout the scriptures, we see prayer in many forms, prayers of faith, praise, supplication, travail, petition, desperation; prayers for ourselves and intercession for others. We see the prayers of healing and warfare, as well as watchman prayers, prophetic prayers, and apostolic prayers. And the list could go on. The point is, as the ekklesia comes together, there are many types and expressions of prayer. All are needful and valid!

With the sword of the Lord in our mouths, Holy Spirit will lead us into the varied expressions of prayer, praise, intercession, travail, declarations, decrees, and more. The beautifully powerful sounds of prayer rising out of the body of Christ releases the sound of rushing waters like a tumult, attracting the attention of the Lord God and all His heavenly hosts. It also puts fear and dread into the enemy's camp, rendering them confused, scattered, and facing the execution of the defeat that has already been secured through the Cross.

When the corporate body comes together as One, armored with the apostles, prophets, evangelists, pastors, and teachers, the power of the Word of God loosed through the ekklesia looses a force of authority to topple strongholds, defeating the enemy, and setting captives free. Aligning together with Christ's kingdom leadership, surrounded by the truth, righteousness, peace, faith, and salvation of Christ unlocks the power of agreement for conquest.

I'm honored to be a part of the Triumphant Prayer Call for Righteousness in our nation, affectionately known as the 222 Prayer Call. Through these daily prayer calls, we have experienced the power of the ekklesia coming together fully armored with Christ's own armor of kingdom leadership. Over the past couple of years, I began to see this revelation of the corporate armor begin to manifest in some enlightening ways, at least to me.

Each day we gather with a panel of leaders from across the nation, sometimes as many as a dozen or more would be on to give voice to the prayers, declarations, and decrees; other times, it would be four or five, with hundreds and even thousands joining on the call to listen and add the power of their agreement. Over the months, I began noticing the leadership gifting that was coming out of the various hosts. I would hear apostolic truth and order, like generals leading the charge. Then I would hear the sound of the prophets boldly prophesying what God was speaking out of heaven. With others, the sound of the evangelists crying out for and calling in the harvest of souls would resound boldly, causing our eyes to see the harvest all around us more clearly. The heart of the shepherd would tenderly and with undeniable strength encourage and draw in the weary, the discouraged, and the wounded, pouring oil upon the heads of all, releasing refreshing, drawing all back into the fold. The insights and understanding of the teacher have come forth time and time again to keep us firmly established in the Word of God, adding strength, confidence, and greater authority as the teachers substantiated by the Word of God the prophetic revelations and utterances.

With all of these leadership grace-gifts operating together by the Spirit of God with honor one for another, the declarations, decrees, and prayers continue to grow stronger day after day. Holy Spirit continually amazes me as He places on each one what is needful to bring forth, and each part fits perfectly together, forming an expression of the corporate armor of God around the assembled ekklesia on the call.

The fruit of this has been increasing maturity among all the people; greater clarity of what God is doing on the earth as we gain a greater revelation of what His eternal purposes are (gaining a more vertical perspective and not tossed to and fro by the horizontal swirl that is around us all); amazing oneness of agreement and testimonies of breakthrough in individuals, families, and regions. The corporate armor in place has released a greater corporate anointing filled with the authority of Christ and His kingdom.

Out of the strength of the five-fold anointing making up the corporate armor, clarity, precision, accuracy, and strength comes forth as the sword. As the sword of the spirit is lifted by the assembled body, with a oneness of sound and in the power of agreement, angel armies pay attention and move forth to perform the word of the Lord. The sword divides and separates, cuts one way to heal and another way to deliver. It cuts through, demolishing the walls of enemy resistance, making a way for the gospel of the kingdom to advance throughout the land.

When the ekklesia stands up together, fully armored with Christ's leadership graces operational in His choice servants, the power to wield the sword of the Spirit with all manner of prayer carries a greater force of authority and power to accomplish God's purposes on the earth.

As we continue to grow and mature in our understanding and function corporately with all of Christ's leadership graces in place, I am convinced we will witness incredible breakthroughs of victory to see people, families, regions, and nations transformed by the power of God.

QUESTIONS FOR YOUR CONSIDERATION

I. Consider the complementary contrast of kings and priests, and express in your own words how you see yourself moving in both of these roles in your walk with God.

II. Ask the Lord to show you times where you have seen the power of agreement in the corporate expression, with the grace-gifts of Christ's leadership releasing greater clarity, direction, and authority as all came into the power of agreement.

III. What hindrances do you see a need to overcome for the body of Christ to move into greater measures of the corporate armor to wield the sword of the Spirit with all prayer more effectively?

A PRAYER FOR YOU TO PRAY

Father God,

I stand amazed at the brilliance of Your ways and Your plans for us, as the body of Christ, to accomplish Your eternal purposes. Christ, thank You for giving to us apostles, prophets, evangelists, pastors, and teachers; for the privilege of aligning with the armor of Your protection through these leaders; and for the supply You have granted them that connects and strengthens what You have given to each one of us. We are truly stronger together than apart! I choose to 'take up the full armor', aligning and agreeing with You and together with others take up the sword of the Spirit and with all prayer release prayers, declarations, and decrees of faith to see Your kingdom purposes established and advanced on earth according to Your divine will. Teach me, and teach us all, how to more fully move as One according to what You have intended from the beginning for Your glory alone. In Jesus' name.

Amen.

10 Concluding Thoughts

THE JOURNEY OF PURSUING AN UNDERSTANDING of what Holy Spirit spoke to me so many years ago has gone through many phases and seasons, and I am certain there are more to come! I'm grateful for the delays and restraints that Holy Spirit placed around me over the years that kept this book from being written before now. The restoration of apostles and prophets has produced a transition of our understanding of evangelists, pastor-shepherds, and teachers from a traditional church paradigm into a paradigm of the kingdom. This process produced lots of phases and expressions of understanding, not only in me but in the body of Christ.

In this process, God has been removing old ways of thinking and viewing leadership, delivering us from hierarchical structures that contain, restrict, and control, and into those set to lay foundations and serve in order to see the saints released to do the works of ministry God has ordained for them. Some of the old ways had been so intrinsically woven into the fabric of church culture that it has taken a lot of shaking, stripping, and reordering to root it out so that God's order could be more fully manifested. That process continues, but we are making significant progress and are set on a course of ever-increasing restoration of all God intended. Hallelujah!

My prayer is that, as you have read, studied and prayed through what I have shared within these pages, you have been filled with hope and courage to pursue everything God has ordained for you. As I know many have suffered and experienced all types of "leadership wounds," I sincerely pray that this revelation brings healing and liberation and that He leads you into His ordained place for you to be aligned for greater fullness of the gifting, calling, and assignments.

For leaders who have given me the honor of having you read these pages, I pray for you, even as I pray for myself, that we would truly be those who carry the heart of the Father, the grace of Christ, and the anointing of Holy Spirit to lead well in humility, grace, wisdom, revelation, strength, and hope. I am convinced that no true leader ever seeks to "lord it over" others, but realize that far too often it has been the ways we have seen, experienced, and learned from, and we have been shaped by systems and structures that had been affected over the last two thousand years of hierarchical structures. But God is delivering and bringing us into wisdom and revelation to lead His way, as Jesus said in Mark 10:42-45:

"Calling them to Himself, Jesus said to them, "You know that those who are recognized as rulers of the Gentiles domineer over them; and their people in high position exercise authority over them. But it is not this way among you; rather, whoever wants to become prominent among you shall be your servant; and whoever wants to be first

Concluding Thoughts

among you shall be slave of all. For even the Son of Man did not come to be served, but to serve, and to give His life as a ransom for many."

God has called us to lead in such a way that all those who put their faith in Christ will walk in the fullness of all He created them to be and do. As those redeemed by the Blood of the Lamb and filled with the very Spirit of God, we have been granted authority to enter boldly into the throne of grace (ref. Hebrews 4:16), to trample on the enemy, to lay hands on the sick, cast out devils, and so much more, all because of Jesus! Hallelujah! We have been clothed and armored with Christ, who is truth, righteousness, peace, faith, and salvation. Through Christ, we have been: made the righteousness of God in Christ Jesus (ref. 2 Corinthians 5:21); given everything we need for life and godliness through Him (ref. 2 Peter 1:3); endued with power from on high (ref. Luke 24:49, Acts 2) and granted the power of Holy Spirit to be and do all that God, our Father, has purposed.

This morning as I was praying and waiting upon the Lord, Holy Spirit began to speak these words to me, and I sensed these words were important for us to fully move into all God has purposed for us, individually and corporately, in taking up the sword of the Spirit and all prayer to advance in power against the enemy.

I desire that My people focus upon Who I am, what I have done, who I say they are, and what I have ordained that they do—and not focus on the sin, failures, shortcomings, traumas, and losses of their lives, past or present, and fear not the future and what lies ahead.

Step into My life-flow.

Walk out of the trap of the enemy to ensnare you by fear, doubt, and unbelief; by shame, accusations, and condemnations; of unworthiness, ideas of not measuring up or not being good enough.

Walk into My supply—onto My path of life; under My canopy of glory. Submerge into and be saturated with the abundance of all I have for you. Everything you need for life and godliness is in you because I am in you and My Word declares that you already have everything you need in Christ Jesus, your Lord.

These words are the reality of the simplicity of the gospel, and yet far too often too many find themselves shrinking back from the very life, power, and authority that Christ purchased at the Cross. No sin, no trauma, no failure is greater than the power of the Cross.

This is true for us individually because of the finished work of the Cross and the power of Christ's resurrection. Because this is true, we are well-able to pick up the sword of the Spirit and to pray in confident assurance, knowing God hears and answers!

Now, if this is true personally, and we know it is, then how much more as we come together as one body, properly fit and knit together with "each joint supplying" (Ephesians 4:16; 2:21), in the unity of the Spirit in the bond of peace (ref. Ephesians 4:3), and living stones built together as God's spiritual house (ref. 1 Corinthians 2:5). We are truly stronger together than we are apart!

As we come together as the body of Christ, fully armored with that which God has given to us as expressions of Christ's leadership: grace-gifts of apostles, prophets, evangelists, pastors, and teachers, the strength and protection of Christ is activated throughout the body. The kingdom leaders are to "supply" according to who Christ has commissioned them to be as His own representatives on the earth. As we put on (or accept and embrace) those Christ has given as apostles, prophets, evangelists, pastors, and teachers, as the corporate armor, what they are intended to supply becomes available for the whole body. Can you see it? Who Christ gave them to be becomes the supply for us all to be thoroughly equipped for every good work and to advance victoriously against the kingdom of darkness.

Could it be that the weakness and vulnerability of the body of Christ that has led to defeat, discouragement, dismemberment, disease, and so much more is due to our lack of embracing and putting on the full armor of God corporately? I am convinced of the Lord that it is. And, I am thoroughly convicted of the Spirit that this is one key to the body of Christ being able to "take up the sword of the Spirit and with all prayer" and advance victoriously against the enemy.

FINAL PRAYER

Father, in the name of Jesus,

I thank You for the Spirit of Wisdom and Revelation that continually leads us into truth and spiritual understanding for the times in which we are living. Grant that we might be among those who demonstrate and reveal the purity, passion, and power of Christ in and through all that we do as we seek to make Your name famous throughout the earth. Teach us, Lord, how to truly move as one, fully armored with the corporate armor You have given so that Your kingdom might be advanced throughout all the earth. Let us truly be a pure representation of You, moving with You to see the kingdom of God come on earth as it is in heaven.

Amen.

About the Author

JACQUIE TYRE IS THE FOUNDER and apostolic leader of CityGate Atlanta and Kairos Transformation Ministries. Raised in a solid Christian home, godly parents and grandparents provided her with a solid foundation in the Word of God and knowledge of God. In 1988, after several years of physical challenges, hospitalizations, complicated pregnancies, and other struggles, Jacquie had a dramatic encounter with the Lord that forever changed her path. Holy Spirit asked, "Are you tired of living life your way?" To which she answered, "YES! My way stinks!"

That moment began a journey of moving from a life of faithfully following Christ to a never-ending adventure of living in communion with the Lord as the lover of her soul and the ever-present teacher, guide, and very source of her life.

Jacquie's early years of serving in the church included participating in worship teams, teaching Sunday School, women's Bible studies, leading outreach ministries, volunteering at a maternity home, and many other activities. Later the emphasis turned increasingly toward intercession and spiritual warfare. Out of her passion for prayer and intercession, she served with numerous organizations, providing leadership, training, mobilizing, and equipping the Body of Christ to take up prayer and intercession, not as a side activity, but as the foundational work for all we are to be and do.

Jacquie carries a passion for revival, awakening, and reformation that compels her to train, equip, mobilize and send people out to fulfill their God-given purpose and destiny. In 2010, God led her to found CityGate Atlanta as an apostolic kingdom center to steward her heart's call, purpose, and vision. The ministry work at CityGate Atlanta and assignments into the nation and nations keeps her busy and living God's dream for her life.

Jacquie is the author of two prayer guides, *The Jabez Prayer Guide* and *Ready for Revival*. She has been happily married to Mike since 1977. They have three wonderful sons with wonderful wives who have made Mike and Jacquie the proud grandparents of four fabulous grandchildren.

Contact Info

Jacquie Tyre Ministries

www.jacquietyre.com
Email: infojtministries@gmail.com

CityGate Atlanta
3100 Medlock Bridge Rd,
Suite 110
Peachtree Corners, GA 30071

Made in the USA
Monee, IL
24 September 2021

78264697R10085